AN ACCIDENTAL

BOOKSELLER

First published in 2019 by Puxley Productions Ltd..

This is a work of nonfiction. Any similarity between the characters and situations within its pages, and places, persons, or animals living or dead, could be unintentional and co-incidental. Some names and identifying details have been changed or omitted to, in part, protect the privacy of individuals.

The right of Bill Samuel to be identified as the author of this work has been asserted by him in accordance with sections 77 and 78 of the Copyright, Designs and Patents Act, 1988.

British Library Cataloguing in Publication Data.
A catalogue record for this book is available from the British Library.

ISBN: 978-1-9160782-1-5 (paperback)

Typeset in Berling
Printed and bound by Ingram Spark in the UK.

Cover Design and typesetting by Jamie Keenan.

AN ACCIDENTAL
BOOKSELLER

A Personal Memoir of
FOYLES

BILL SAMUEL

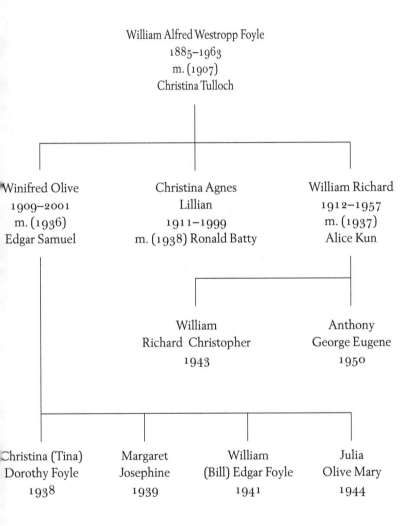

William Alfred Westropp Foyle
1885–1963
m. (1907)
Christina Tulloch

Winifred Olive
1909–2001
m. (1936)
Edgar Samuel

Christina Agnes
Lillian
1911–1999
m. (1938) Ronald Batty

William Richard
1912–1957
m. (1937)
Alice Kun

William
Richard Christopher
1943

Anthony
George Eugene
1950

Christina (Tina)
Dorothy Foyle
1938

Margaret
Josephine
1939

William
(Bill) Edgar Foyle
1941

Julia
Olive Mary
1944

'For many years I lived in India, and one of the highlights of my visits to London was the moment I stepped into Foyles. It was the closest feeling I could remember to having sixpence to spend in a sweetie-shop, a place with more books than I could imagine under one roof. I knew I would find the one I was after and many more I didn't know I needed. (Maybe I am imagining this, but I think there were so many books they jostled off the shelves and came right out on to the street to waylay the reader.) On rainy days it was the perfect place to be, in the warren of aisles where the books breathed and ruffled their pages. I spent hours browsing, because I couldn't afford all the ones I wanted, but no-one seemed to mind and Foyles knew books don't get used up by being read. The day I found my own book of poems on the shelf was one of the best days of my life. I still walk into Foyles and turn my front covers to face the world. I suppose the staff just sigh and put them back, knowing another vandal poet has been in.'

Imtiaz Dharker

'I have very fond memories of Foyles. I remember it was one of my first ports of call when I moved to London in 1987, no job, nowhere to live and the grand total of £12 in my pocket. I remember the old system of paying for a book and receiving a ticket, which you had to take to another desk to collect your purchase. I would have liked to have applied for a job there but was too intimidated by somewhere that seemed unreachably grand and famous a place for the likes of me. Having not a penny to my name in my early days in London (I lived in a squat and worked as a part-time secretary), I could rarely afford to buy books anyway, but spent many a happy hour browsing and getting lost in what seemed to be endless nooks and crannies.

I also remember it moving to its current premises - I went to the opening party as a published author and rubbed shoulders with the likes of Stanley Tucci. I've bought books there, done events there - and it has a special place in my heart as one of the last places I visited with my great friend Andrea Levy, who died in February this year.'

Louise Doughty

'I was based in the West End in the early eighties, when Foyles was at its eccentric finest, with a truly freestyle selection of books and an anachronistic method of payment that required sturdy shoes and a fine sense of direction. The bookstore also had an excellent history section, the stock ordered, I supposed, by a history professor with more than a passing taste for things military. I was on a meagre salary at the time - barely £70 a week - so the £21 cover price of an excellent book on the Desert Campaign of WW2 was well outside my pocket. This being Foyles, however, where oddball behaviour was not shunned but actively encouraged, I opted to read the book during successive lunchtimes while perched on a pile of remaindered Churchill biographies. No-one seemed the least put out and I carried on like this for a week. Alas, my carefully laid plan was scuppered when some unbelievable rotter bought the book I was reading, so I never did find out how the Desert Campaign ended. If anyone knows, a postcard with the final score written theron would be most welcome.

There are bookshops - and then there is Foyle's.'

Jasper Fforde

'In the 1970s, entering Foyles was like returning to a huge version of the bookshops of my childhood, in Colombo: a mysterious, perplexing, arcane repository of the unexpected.

But my best memory is from 2006. The shop had been transformed: locatable books, jazz and coffee, an events space. Upstairs an exhibition of Sri Lankan books had been organised and I did a reading at the opening. The political scene in Sri Lanka was tense, but perhaps those multiple stories of books buoyed us all. Conversations bubbled and led to the development of two new literary festivals: one at Asia House in London, and the other in Galle, Sri Lanka. Both still going, and much needed, as I hope Foyles will keep going to feed the needs of readers whatever the challenges ahead.'

Romesh Gunesekera

'The first time I heard about Foyles was early in the 1960s when I was a teenager at Charterhouse, and a young aspiring writer, and my English teacher told me that during WW2, Christina Foyle had lined the roof of the bookstore with copies of Adolf Hitler's *Mein Kampf*. I just loved this story - it really touched something in me - and I so hoped it was true - and subsequently found it was! Then two decades later as a published but very much midlist author, I used to read about the legendary literary lunches and dream that one day I would be invited to one. Sadly my rise from the midlist came too late. But at least one dream had come true - to see my books on their hallowed shelves. For me the name Foyles will forever signify so much that is wonderful about the world of books. Humour, defiance, courage and the endless riches that the printed page bestows upon humankind.'

Peter James

Amid all the algorithms and cookies, the metadata and SEO, Foyles has steadfastly continued doing what it has always done so well: introducing brilliant books to readers of all ages and all backgrounds. Long may it continue.'

Clare Mackintosh

'I've loved Foyles since reading about it in other people's books. In 'Not That Sort of Girl' by Mary Wesley, Rose consults a sex manual in the lavatory in Foyles. I was still living in a village in Yorkshire then and it seemed the height of glamour. When I moved to London it was a delight to go and browse the actual shelves and it is still one of my favourite things to lose myself without objective and come out a couple of hours later with a book I didn't know I wanted. I was once asked out in the foreign languages department and have had many happy hours chatting or people watching in the cafes in both the old and new buildings. It is a joy to interview authors there as the space is so welcoming, the booksellers so efficient, and the audiences so keen. Foyles truly is an oasis, a good deed in a naughty world, a beacon of hope and all that is good.'

Cathy Rentzenbrink

'When I met Bill I found a friend who was deeply committed to human rights. He understood the importance of denouncing social injustices through the medium of social documentary photography and supported a number of exhibitions of my work in Foyles Gallery and the launch of my poetry book, *Oranges in Times of Moon*, in 2006.

Bill and Foyles had the courage to show an exhibition which challenged the perception of the people of Iraq disseminated by the media. Iraq: The People, launched a few days before the allied invasion of Iraq in March 2003, revealed a people living together in a peaceful society who were suffering the consequences of twelve years of economic sanctions imposed by the west.

I know that the exhibitions had an impact on the public from the feedback we received and played a part in changing perceptions on the causes of global poverty.'

Carlos Reyes Manzo

'When I was a little girl my biggest treat during the Christmas holidays was a trip to Foyles Bookshop in the Charing Cross Road. I was allowed to select my Christmas present book in the Children's Section. We had a W.H. Smith's back home in Kingston-on-Thames – but even at the age of seven I knew perfectly well that Foyles was the real deal, the King of all the bookshops in the country.

I spent a long time browsing the bookshelves because choosing was part of the treat. I was ages wondering whether I wanted another Faraway Tree book or a Mary Poppins or the latest Noel Streatfeild. When I eventually unwrapped my choice on Christmas Day the little green book sticker saying Foyles inside the cover was definitely part of the thrill.

As I got older I loved the large second-hand book section. It was such a joy to read a novel by Elizabeth Jane Howard and then discover pristine first editions on the second-hand shelves, all at half price.

When I became a writer myself I was thrilled to see my own books on the shelves, and I loved it when I was asked to do events at the shop. Bill made such an impact when he became involved.

His memoir has brought back so many marvellous memories and reminded me of the chaos and confusion of the shop under the indomitable Christina's regime. I never met her, but my daughter did. She hoped to get a Saturday job at Foyles whilst studying for her A-levels. She suffered the fate of many at her interview. She knocked at Christina's door and walked in timidly, fresh-faced and smartly dressed. Christina apparently shook her head at the sight of her and said one word: 'No!' '

Jacqueline Wilson

Contents

Introduction 1

1 William 7

2 Christina 29

3 The Shop 49

4 Fridays at the Shop 53

5 Me 59

6 The Book Trade 73

7 Taking Stock 79

8 Development 95

9 Personal Memories 117

10 All Good Things... 133

11 Exit 141

Epilogue 145

Acknowledgements 151

INTRODUCTION

IN THE CLOSING MONTHS OF the twentieth century Christina Foyle decided it was her time to die. After eighty-nine years dictating the terms upon which she lived she presumably saw no reason not to do the same with her death. At the beginning of June 1999, living in an old abbey in Essex with mainly cats for company, she stopped eating and drinking and was dead within ten days. I am an accountant, trained in bookkeeping, not bookselling, but to my considerable surprise some months later I found myself helping to run our family business, W & G Foyle Ltd, Foyles bookshop.

Some sixty years earlier I had chosen my grandparents with great care: a classless couple from south-east London, vaudeville entertainers from whom, as birth presents, I inherited a love of music and a modest desire to perform; and an East End couple, she a convent-brought-up Scottish orphan, he a bookseller, also in his own way a showman – their birth presents to me were a passion for books and an acceptance of others for what they are, not whence they come.

From this inherited framework I navigated a zigzag path through life which took me from Surrey via Denmark, Africa, the Middle East and the Caribbean, to Charing Cross Road and the board of a much-loved but dying family business.

All my life I have been interested in family businesses. Since the industrial revolution they have been, and remain, the backbone of the economies of most countries. Some of them, a very few, grow enough to move on and become quoted companies, whereupon they lose their distinct character; their ongoing purpose becomes the payment of dividends to the shareholders and the relationship between the owners and the employees changes. Some continue in family ownership for many generations. Most fall by the wayside after a few years or decades, clogs to clogs in three generations. The atmosphere within a family business is subtly different from that of a quoted company or part of a conglomerate. The owners are more likely to take a personal interest in the company and to have direct contact with and interest in the staff. There is more likely to be dedication to the process of the business than the profit arising from it. My family's business, Foyles, is the subject of this memoir.

Christina Foyle left behind her a bookshop of almost unbelievable idiosyncrasy, a strange mixture of charm, frustration and eccentricity. She had been the undisputed head of the business for nearly fifty years and an influence on her father William Foyle for many years before that. She was there in its heyday and oversaw its subsequent long slow slide into gentle chaos. The business was four years shy of its hundredth birthday and in almost terminal decline.

Christina was my aunt, William my maternal grandfather. This is not a history of Foyles or a biography of William or Christina. It is a very personal memoir of my relationships with a wonderful family business and with two extraordinary people. It is memories from childhood mingled with recent events and discoveries. It is subjective, personal, partial and incomplete. Some memories are blurred by the passage of time, some sharpened by nostalgia, and others changed by the subconscious from the actuality into what I would have liked things to have been. This account is a combination of all those; it is, as they say, 'my truth' and as such it is the story I want to tell before my memories of the main characters are too blurred by my own old age.

*   *   *

My maternal family, the Foyles, have an entrepreneurial streak which has passed down the generations. My great-great-grandfather George Foyle was butler to Sir Thomas McMahon, the Lieutenant Governor of Portsmouth, who had paid for his education. In 1843 George and his family left Portsmouth for Hoxton, in the East End of London and, drawing on his experience below stairs in the general's household, set up in business as Foyle & Co., a wholesale grocer and dry-salter, preserving meats for butchers, in the days long before refrigeration. My great-grandfather William, who was his seventh child, married Deborah Barnett, daughter of Jewish immigrants from Eastern Europe, and eventually took over the family business. As the business was only large enough to support one family, it was earmarked for their oldest son, also called George: their other five sons left school at sixteen to make their own way in the world.

The family's business only survived one more generation, but four of the other sons built up businesses which would outlast it by many decades. The second son Charlie invented and patented the folding cardboard carton, building up a substantial company, Boxfoldia, in Birmingham. Another son became a furniture retailer, eventually selling out to one of the largest retailers in mid-twentieth-century England, Isaac Wolfson's Great Universal Stores. The two youngest brothers set up Foyles bookshop.

What became in its heyday indisputably the world's greatest bookshop grew from a modest pile of unwanted textbooks on my great-grandmother's kitchen table. William and Gilbert, the fifth and sixth sons, decided on careers in the

3

Civil Service. In order to study for the entrance examinations they had to buy textbooks. When they eventually failed the exams they advertised the books for sale and were so impressed with the response that they bought more to resell, initially colonizing their mother's kitchen for their business premises. They bought books wherever they could find them – in the salerooms, from students, from private individuals and from second-hand bookshops. They collected and delivered on bicycles; one of the earliest photos I have of them is on a tandem in 1903, although as it doesn't appear to have any carrying capacity I suspect that it was taken as a very early publicity shot.

After six months they opened their first second-hand bookshop in Peckham and a couple of years later moved to Cecil Court, off Charing Cross Road, the heart of London's bookselling. Within a few more years they had outgrown those premises and moved to Charing Cross Road itself, against the advice of friends who told them there were too many bookshops there already. William Foyle lived for, and surrounded himself by, books. He seldom forgot a title. He went to endless trouble to track down unusual or rare books. From the start Foyles earned a reputation for being able to supply books on even the most out-of-the-way subjects and the business prospered. Within a decade or so they were the largest of Charing Cross Road's many bookshops, boasting a stock of over a million books.

He realized early on that the secret was not just to have as many books in stock as the premises would hold, but to make those premises inviting to the ordinary man and woman. In the early days the books were all second-hand, so the cost was low and a certain amount of theft could be accepted. Archive photographs show books on shelves outside the shop, customers browsing out in the street. Most bookshops at the time were quiet, dark, uninviting places; Foyles at its first Charing Cross Road premises declared: 'Come and look, the books may be second-hand and slightly tatty but they contain all the knowledge of the world.'

In the 1920s the business moved into the premises which, when I was growing up, were known in the family simply as The Shop, one of the cornerstones of my childhood, a magical place where I learnt to love books. It sat on nearly half an acre on the edge of Soho, fronting onto Charing Cross Road and straddling Manette Street, with an annex on the north side which housed paperbacks and theology, and included the lovely Artists House, once a Victorian workhouse but from the mid 1930s the home of Foyles Book Clubs. Foyles, by then advertising itself as 'The World's Greatest Bookshop', had become a great sprawling rabbit warren of books and book-related activities employing some 350 people, with an annual turnover the equivalent of nearly £100 million at today's values and still dominated by William.

I had been told as a young child that my grandfather owned the largest second-hand bookshop in the world. By the tender age of four I had already absorbed some conventional middle-class values and felt ever so slightly ashamed of this – there was a stigma attached to 'second-hand' and I would have preferred to have had a grandad with a 'new' bookshop. Of course, when I saw for the first time the vastness of the place and found it had more books than I could possibly imagine, I simply thought *Wow!* And I've thought *Wow!* ever since. My mother before me had felt the same. When she was very young, not too long after the business transferred to its first premises in Charing Cross Road, she stood outside the main entrance telling all those coming in or out, 'I'm Daddy's little girl!'

Foyles was, and remained for three generations, a family business. After working together for twenty years the founders, William and Gilbert, by then both married with families of their own, divided the company into two separate businesses, with Gilbert taking the majority shareholding in Foyles Educational Ltd, supplying schools and colleges, and William keeping the retail business, W & G Foyle Ltd. William was later joined by my mother Winifred, my aunt Christina and my uncle Dick; Gilbert by his sons Eric and John. Foyles remained in family ownership for 115 years.

Shortly before Christina died my cousin Christopher Foyle joined the board and on her death became chairman. As the third chairman he guided Foyles with a light touch through the turbulent waters of early twenty-first-century bookselling and oversaw the rebirth of the company. His brother Anthony was made a director a few months later and helped uncover some of the frauds which were rampant at Foyles towards the end of Christina's life, enabling the company to prosecute the manager and assistant manager and make room for new management. I was the third member of the third generation to join the board. This is a memoir of my involvement.

1. WILLIAM

WILLIAM FOYLE, 'GRANDAD', WAS BORN in a terraced house in Curtain Road, Shoreditch, in the East End of London in 1885. (According to Charles Booth's fascinating survey of 1889, *Life and Labour of the People*, Curtain Road at the time was inhabited mainly by those with 'Intermittent earnings, 18s to 21s per week for a moderate family. Labourers, poorer artisans and street sellers,' with small pockets of 'Lowest Class. Vicious, Semi-criminal'.) He died seventy-eight years later in a beautiful twelfth-century abbey with several hundred acres of land, one of the finest private libraries in the world and a Rolls-Royce in the garage.

During those seventy-eight years he possibly did more to put books into the hands of ordinary people than anyone had done before, through his labyrinthine bookshop in Charing Cross Road with its thirty miles of shelving and world-wide mail-order business, through his book clubs distributing tens of millions of books to half a million members over their fifty-year history and through his lending libraries with their three thousand agents spread as far as Palestine, India and Australia. The only public recognition he ever received was to be made a Commander of the Order of the Red Cross of Estonia, having funded the construction of a hospital there when he read that they were unable to cope with an epidemic of tuberculosis. One day a biography may be written. This is not it.

He was born a cockney and never lost his cockney accent. Of medium height and more than medium girth, he had long silver hair curling on his shoulders, twinkling eyes and a ready laugh. He smoked Havana cigars and carried their aroma around with him. He was warm and generous and fun and a great influence on my early life. He was also knowledgeable and intelligent and encouraged us to enquire and question. We would see him regularly either in the Shop or at his beautiful house, Beeleigh Abbey, just west of Maldon, in Essex.

On leaving school at sixteen William worked briefly as a clerk for Sir Edward Marshall Hall, a prominent criminal barrister and a collector of antique silver. William was occasionally sent to salesrooms, where he developed a love of interesting books. This employment did not last long, William's early deafness making it hard for him to follow court proceedings, so he and his younger brother Gilbert decided to sit the Civil Service examinations, their failure in which lead to the establishment of Foyles.

William was still only nineteen when, on one of his book-buying trips to a shop in New Oxford Street, he met and fell in love with Christina Tulloch, an orphaned and convent-educated descendant of seafaring folk from the Shetland Islands. Thinking him a poor student, she let him have the books he sought very cheaply. He was trying to find a copy of Xenophon's *Anabasis* which she, with only a basic nineteenth-century convent education, struggled to pronounce, let alone to read. She was some three years older than William and their backgrounds were very different, but with the blessing of her guardian, Captain (later Admiral Sir Richard) Webb, they married in 1907 and by 1912 they had had their three children. The oldest was Winifred, my mother; Christina, my Auntie Chrissie, was eighteen months younger; Richard, my Uncle Dick, the youngest. To my mother and I believe to Dick, William was an adoring and attentive father, to Christina he was a distant and authoritative business man. I recall my mother, after reading a memoir written by Christina, saying: 'I think we had different parents.' William's children all married in the late 1930s and eventually produced six grandchildren: my three sisters Tina, Margaret and Julie and me, and Dick's two sons Christopher and Anthony.

William was a great innovator and Foyles during his reign was a constantly evolving business. Second-hand books led on to new books, to publishing, to book clubs and to library supply. Educational books led to educational film production and to a separate company, Foyles Educational Ltd. Books about music led on to sheet music, to recorded music and eventually to musical instruments, sold from a separate shop in Charing Cross Road. Peripheral activities included a gallery, lecture and entertainment agencies, a travel bureau, a chain of lending libraries across several continents and a significant property portfolio eventually of far more value than the bookselling business.

In 1927 Foyles' in-house magazine *Foylibra* printed the following under 'My Aims as a Bookseller' by W. A. Foyle:

1. To supply almost any Book, in print or out of print.

2. To supply the greatest number of Books to the greatest number of people and consequently to have a Bookshop equipped with –

3. A staff of specially trained men and women, all busy radiating knowledge, cheerfulness and politeness.

4. To have premises at least 100 feet long and 100 feet wide and, say, 50 feet high, with a gallery round and a glass dome roof similar to Cole's Great Book Arcade in Melbourne, Australia.

5. To encourage people to buy and possess Books so that it would be almost a disgrace for an intelligent person not to

have a small library and not to be fairly well read.

6. To persuade the whole of the Book Trade to organize for the furtherance of the object of paragraph 5.

7. To organize literary functions, dinners etc., where people interested in literature can see and hear well-known authors as was done fifty or so years ago.

8. To persuade the Booksellers and kindred Associations to issue millions of copies of a booklet for every member of the community to have, extolling the pleasures and advantages of Book Reading.

9. To live long enough to do all these things and not to forget them in the day-to-day detail of business.

It is worth noting that he capitalizes the word 'Book' throughout. It is also worth noting that Foyles' twenty-first-century premises in the old Central Saint Martins building with its central atrium and galleried first floor accurately reflects William's aim number four. Above the short flight of stairs leading from the atrium down to lifestyle, children's and travel there is the slogan 'Welcome book lover, you are among friends.' Grandad would have approved.

William set up, in the 1920s, Foyle's Welsh Depot (which by August 1930 had become Foyle's Welsh Company Ltd), producing catalogues of new, second-hand and antiquarian books in Welsh and offering 'every Welsh Gramophone record issued' and 'a large assortment of Welsh maps, views and cartoons'. This led on, in 1928, to Gwasg Cymraeg Foyle, publishing books about Wales, in Welsh, and in 1930 to Foyle's Welsh Press (the direct translation of Gwasg Cymraeg Foyle), publishing books of Welsh interest but in English. There was a short-lived venture, Foylaphone, language courses on vinyl records which tried and failed to compete with Linguaphone, which had a twenty-year head start.

In 1935 he started a separate but wholly owned publishing company, John Gifford Ltd, named, obscurely, after his wife's maternal grandfather, which over several decades published both fiction and non-fiction, including a range of Foyles Handbooks on everything from dog breeding to mushroom growing and which can still be found in quantity in second-hand bookshops. Fiction included some early works by Ursula Bloom; non-fiction, 'Recipes of the 1940s' by the appropriately named Irene Veal.

The medical department sold skeletons in various sizes to medical students and the handicrafts department sold card and raffia, glue and darning needles, wool and knitting supplies. The tide of incoming post from all parts of the world provided the stock for the philately department, with the ladies in the post room instructed to cut all the stamps off the envelopes.

During William's time Foyles became a formidable force in book retailing. When the first public edition of T. E. Lawrence's *Seven Pillars of Wisdom* was published in 1935 Foyles subscribed 7,000 copies, which was, I believe, the largest single book order ever placed in the UK at that time. Underlying every innovation and development in the business was his love of books and his admiration for those who wrote them. In 1948 he instituted the Foyle Poetry Prize, worth £500 to the winner, at the time the most valuable poetry prize in the world. It ran until his death, when Christina decided to discontinue it.

Christened by someone in the trade as 'the Barnum of Bookselling' William understood instinctively that books are entertainment and bookshops had to offer more than just a wide selection of books to keep bringing the customers back. He loved people and he loved the obvious enjoyment that his shop gave them. I have heard that in earlier life he was a driven businessman, spending too little time with his family, but his legacy was a bookshop known with affection throughout the world. I will only remember him as one of the kindest, most generous people I have ever met, an inspiration to me and to many others.

*　　*　　*

From very early on he showed an interest in the welfare of the staff. Another of the early archive photographs I have is of the annual company picnic in 1912, with thirty staff posing slightly stiffly in what then passed for casual clothing, my three-year-old mother sitting in front with their St Bernard dog. When my mother began working at the shop in 1928 she was tasked with setting up and running a social club for the staff, which she continued to do for some years and through which she eventually met my father. In the mid 1930s William bought a six-bedroomed Georgian farmhouse out in Essex for the staff to use at weekends and on holidays, which Christina eventually sold as she thought the staff weren't treating it with enough respect.

As an entrepreneur William was unusual in combining the skills of an innovator with those of an enabler. In 1930 Christina, aged nineteen, suggested that it would be good to have a forum where readers could meet writers. William said it sounded like a good idea and told her to go ahead and set something up, which was the birth of the Foyles Literary Luncheons. These continued unbroken into the twenty-first century, more than seven hundred luncheons spanning seventy years.

When, in 1936, Victor Gollancz set up the Left Book Club my father suggested, over a pint in the Pillars of Hercules pub, that Foyles should set up a right-wing equivalent. Grandad, typically, said okay, you do it, so Dad set up the Foyles Book Clubs, which eventually had half a million members each receiving a book a month. By the time they were discontinued in the 1980s they had sold more than seventy million books, the cashflow from which enabled the company to build up the property portfolio that underpinned the finances of the bookshop until the early years of the twenty-first century.

Like most entrepreneurs William had his ups and downs and at times he was dependent on his bank for support. One

Friday he needed to cash a cheque for wages, but the bank cashier told him there were insufficient funds and sent him into the manager's office. The manager was uncooperative. William said, 'But today is my birthday.' The manager replied, 'I still can't give you cash, but I can buy you lunch.' They went off for a very convivial lunch, possibly to his favourite restaurant above The Horseshoe pub just up Tottenham Court Road. They returned obviously in good spirits and William gave the cashier a 'thumbs up' behind the back of the manager, who disappeared into his office. William claimed the cash from a gullible cashier and the next Monday received a furious phone call from the manager: 'William, I see from my diary that your birthday was last March.' But too late, the wages had been paid.

It was a time when banks had a different and much more personal approach to customer service. The day that Barclays Bank opened its new branch at 5 Oxford Street, in the late 1930s, Foyles and all adult members of the Foyle family opened accounts there. When I was twelve I did so too and continued to bank there for thirty years, the doorman calling me 'Mr. Billy' well into my adult life. During the years I lived overseas one of my first calls on the rare occasions I was back in the UK on leave was, of course, to the bank. I remember on several occasions asking to be put through to the assistant manager with whom I dealt: after a slight pause the telephone operator would ask, 'Is that Mr Samuel?' I found out he was blind and had an extraordinary memory for voices.

Customer service has changed, perhaps not for the better, but banks still rely on customers' reluctance to move their accounts. When, after becoming involved in the company, I started to look into Foyles' banking arrangements I found that Barclays, our bankers for nearly a century, were charging us 3% on credit-card transactions. I phoned them to say that this was extortionate and they offered to reduce it to 2%. I shopped around, had an offer from Lloyds of 1¼% and moved our substantial accounts. The Barclays area director called me and when I told him why we had left them he said,

'But we would have reduced to 1¼%.'

I said, 'What a shame for Barclays that you didn't.'

William was the undisputed head of the business from the early 1920s when he and Gilbert divided the business into two separate companies, until the late 1940s when he officially handed over control to Christina, although he continued to maintain his office on the second floor and to influence the business for another decade or more. In the early 1950s he decided to give his shares to his children to avoid death duties, now called inheritance taxes. He was of the firm belief that control of a family business should be in the hands of one person, his views perhaps coloured by the strategy differences which he had had with his brother Gilbert during the decades that they worked together as equal partners, so he gave some 60% to Christina, his obvious successor. To Dick, working full-time in the business, he gave half the amount Christina got and to my mother 1,000 shares, approximately 8%. She was no longer working in the business and was married to a man who was at best unreliable with money. This small shareholding gave my mother sufficient income to support our family but not enough to encourage my father in his business ventures. Dick died a year or two later, leaving his shares equally to his two sons. This division of shares resulted eventually but inevitably in the sale of this family business some sixty-five years later.

William and Gilbert had started out with no capital and the company has never sought outside investment. Its growth, from a kitchen table to 'the World's Greatest Bookshop' over the space of a few decades, was financed entirely from retained profits. William's extraordinary entrepreneurial talents had created a broadly-based retail business, based on bookselling but embracing so much more. His motivation was not to make money but to make the widest range of books available to the greatest number of people and in doing so he became a rich man.

*   *   *

Until the early 1940s William and his wife Christina lived at Ilfra Lodge, a comfortable detached Victorian house in East Finchley. For recreation, like many from similar East End backgrounds, he would escape to Essex, where he kept a small sailing boat on the upper reaches of the River Crouch, in the village of Fambridge, a little upriver from Burnham. He was a keen rambler and would go for long walks through the flat marshy Essex countryside. On one such walk he came across, and fell in love with, Beeleigh Abbey. He made an offer to the then owner, which was initially refused, but he persisted, and in 1943 his latest offer of £4,000 was accepted. He was, by then, ready to move to a quieter life in the country, to take on the huge commitment which such a purchase entailed and he became the owner of a substantial medieval property in need of major modernization. When I first visited in 1946 it was still partially lit by gas and had no mains water.

Beeleigh was built in the late twelfth century, an important abbey of the Premonstratensian order. Following Henry VIII's second wave of dissolutions of monasteries in 1539, it was sold into private ownership. Many of the original buildings have gone, but what remains is the heart of the old Abbey, the calefactory, or warming room, built round the Abbey's only fireplace and source of heat, the dormitory above and the adjacent chapter house where the important business of the Abbey was discussed. There was a Tudor extension, added shortly after the dissolution to make the Abbey more suitable for family life. By the time William bought it, it was a beautiful and beautifully proportioned country house standing in a dozen or so acres of garden, formal in part but running with increasing informality down to the River Chelmer, still subject to the North Sea tides a mile or so upstream from Maldon.

There is a spring above the house from which the water supply was drawn, which gives birth to a stream running beside the main garden path down to the river and where it joins the river there is a little vantage point jutting out from the muddy bank. William had put a bench there and as children we would sit and watch the river's changing shape and moods. At low tide it is a slow, muddy channel perhaps ten yards wide, moving almost imperceptibly from left to right; it grows with the tide to a majestic waterway thirty yards or more across and, following any heavy rain, to a powerful, swirling torrent sweeping branches and debris down to the sea. Swans drift along its surface, somehow more majestic in the flat Essex countryside than their royal cousins inland on the Thames. It meanders down from Chelmsford, which owes the river its name, through flat farmland, arriving (viewed from the bench) stage left; in front it divides the Beeleigh gardens from the marshlands fringing the Maldon Golf Club; to the right it disappears under a distant Victorian railway bridge to the light industry of Maldon.

The front door to the house is in the corner by the junction of the original Norman building and the beautifully timbered 'new' Tudor extension. From a small lobby inside, a few stone steps lead down to the calefactory, a little over forty feet long by twenty feet wide, its vaulted stone ceiling supported by three Purbeck-marble pillars. To the right a few steps lead up to the small and cosy Tudor living-cum-dining room, where Granny spent much of her day; I suspect the Abbey and its management were quite daunting for her and she found it simpler to sit and read in what was by far the smallest room in the main part of the house. The other end of the calefactory leads through to the chapter house, a room of similar size, also with a vaulted stone ceiling supported by pillars, chipped by the horns of the cattle which a previous owner had once kept there. In the far corner was a hand-pumped organ from the mid eighteenth century, originally gifted to London's Foundling Hospital where it was played frequently by Friedrich Handel. We were told that it was on this organ that Handel composed his *Largo*, a claim to fame shared by a number of similar instruments. Once a month on Sunday evenings in summer there were evensong services, officiated by the vicar of Maldon Parish Church, of which William was a significant benefactor. The congregation would spill out into the beautiful Beeleigh gardens, singing hymns of William's choosing, accompanied by Handel's old hand-pumped organ, the summer perfumes blending with the frankincense which William would burn in a traditional censer.

Upstairs there were six main bedrooms, all with substantial oak four-poster beds, one of which was made for King James I although he never stayed in the house. This bed was in one of the three large bedrooms on the second floor, a room that by reputation was haunted by the ghost of a monk murdered by one of his brothers. In our imagination we saw the ghost many times and we would never venture into the 'James Room' after dark. My sisters and I would lie awake in the adjacent rooms where we usually slept, listening to the wooden stairs creaking as they gave out the heat of the day and imagining a cowled monk creeping upstairs, with that delicious thrill of fear which we knew was unjustified. Our mock fear was mirrored by a nineteenth-century print on the wall of one of the bedrooms entitled 'When tempests roar and timbers creak,' a picture of two small children cowering under the blankets of a four-poster bed. I recall waking before dawn one morning and seeing the ghost of a monk, in a hooded cowl, in my doorway; I lay, terrified, until in the growing light the 'ghost' resolved itself into the heavy curtain hanging over the door – thus are many ghost stories born. But in spite of this, Beeleigh was never a spooky house and for us as children it was a house with endless possibilities for adventure.

Above the calefactory was the old dormitory of the Abbey, nearly fifty feet long by twenty wide, with a beautiful curved timber roof dating back to the thirteenth century. This housed the library which William had built up over many years, one of the finest private libraries in the country, home to some 20,000 books, the range of which reflected William's very broad taste; it included one each of the first four folios editions of Shakespeare, a Caxton, a leaf from a Gutenberg bible and many exquisite illuminated manuscripts from the twelfth century onwards. He had started collecting during his book-buying expeditions, in other second-hand shops and from market stalls, where he once found a first edition of Fitzgerald's translation of *The Rubaiyat of Omar Khayyam* for 2*d* and of one of Dickens's novels for 6*d*. Later he bought from dealers, some of whom became friends, including Philip and Lionel Robinson who had bought, sight unseen, the nineteenth-century Phillips Collection for £100,000 and never had to work again.

Some he bought at country-house auctions, at a time when there was a very active, and illicit, antiquarian book dealers' ring, under the clandestine rules of which only one member would bid at auction, with the books acquired being then auctioned privately between the members, the profit being shared between them. William refused to participate. He claimed to have shared a train to one such auction with members of the ring who, on arrival, took the only available taxi, so he flagged down a passing hearse, bribed the driver to take him as quickly as possible to the venue, where he arrived before the taxi and bought the books he wanted privately. When the other dealers finally arrived he told them how he had beaten them. One said 'and to think that we took our hats off when the hearse went past'.

He bought his particularly fine Third Folio Shakespeare at an auction at Sotheby's in 1947 for £4,400, which was slightly more than he had paid for Beeleigh Abbey with its many acres a few years earlier. It had the initials S.P. on the spine and William always believed it had originally belonged to Samuel Pepys, but Christies have since cast doubt on that. In any event, it was eventually sold after Christina's death for £420,000.

When my mother was eighteen she was browsing her father's library and came across Burton's translation of *One*

Thousand and One Nights. As she dipped into it she thought: what strange things Arab men and women did with each other. On the same shelf she found a translation of Boccaccio's *Decameron*, started reading and thought: that's odd, they seem to have done the same things in medieval Italy. Then the penny dropped and my mother, aged eighteen, learned through classical literature the facts of life.

*   *   *

When we were children, Beeleigh was paradise. My earliest memories are of Christmas 1946, when I was five, the first Christmas after my father had returned from the Middle East where he had finished his wartime service. My parents were there, and possibly my Uncle Dick and his family – certainly there were too many of us to be accommodated at the Abbey, so my youngest sister and I were boarded out with one of the gardeners, Mr Quy, who lived with his wife in a small terraced house on the outskirts of Maldon. It gave me a glimpse of how life used to be: Beeleigh still had gas lights and Mr Quy's house had its privy on the other side of the road on the edge of the fields. At five years old I was charged with taking my little sister, not yet three, across the road in our dressing gowns and pyjamas, before bedtime, in the middle of winter. Each morning Mr Quy would drive us the few miles back to the Abbey and we would warm up by the great fireplace, only used at Christmas when several tons of logs were burned and the heat made it impossible to get closer than several feet away.

Mr Quy was a large, quiet, gentle man, a man of few words but always there lovingly tending the gardens. He was devoted to William. In all the years we were to know him we never learnt his other name; even his wife only ever called him 'Mr Quy'. He was part of Beeleigh throughout our childhood and the last time I saw him was some sixteen years later at Grandad's funeral, as devoted as ever.

We would visit every school holiday, always staying a full week to fit in with the rhythm of William's life: he went into the Shop on Fridays, but only on Fridays. Foyles, by then some 60,000 square feet on both sides of Manette Street and one of the largest bookshops in the world, was always just 'the Shop'. After a day at the Shop and lunch at the Trocadero, mid afternoon we would meet at William's office on the second floor and go down to the goods yard where his chauffeur Joe Little would be waiting with the car. He would drive us out through the East End of London onto the Southend Road, where we would always stop at a pub, the Golden Fleece. William would have a pint, we would have Britvic fruit juices and take a half pint out to Joe waiting in the car.

The publican, Ken Langley, had been a fighter pilot during the war and would regale us with stories of his wartime experiences, of flying his Spitfire wing-tip to wing-tip alongside the V1 'doodlebugs' to try and tip them over. As I write this I remember that the then licensing hours would not have allowed Ken to serve beer mid-afternoon, but my memories are quite clear so I suspect that the licensing laws were bent a little for William. After half an hour or so we would set off again, Grandad dozing through the second half of the journey, we excited to catch the first glimpse of Beeleigh's red-tiled roof through the trees. The car would crunch to a halt by the front door and from the little lobby inside we would descend the few stone steps down to the calefactory. We would breath in the air of the Abbey, tap the large dinner gong by the foot of the stairs, run up the steps on the right leading to the little dining room where our grandmother, never really comfortable in this rather grand house, felt most at home. She would greet us slightly formally, not having the relaxed acceptance of children which William had.

At Beeleigh William had a fairly fixed routine. Breakfast, prepared by the cook in the large kitchen at the other end of the house, would be served to us in the dining room; this was not an age when breakfast would have been eaten in the kitchen. He would then spend the morning working in his study, dealing with the small sack of post sent down each week by his secretary Miss Wyman, or in his library dealing with his books – the library was an ever-changing collection, added to, pruned and replaced. Although he was as generous with his time as he was with his money we generally didn't disturb him there. Once I did go in and I saw him taking envelopes from a pile on his desk and putting a ten-shilling note into each. When I asked him why, he explained that every week he received many begging letters and that while he knew that most of them were fraudulent he always sent them ten shillings so he wouldn't miss the few that were genuine.

We would play bowls and croquet in the afternoons, which were, of course, always sunny, and cards and dominoes in the evening. He used to cheat outrageously, but somehow one of us always won. Sometimes we would go fishing, walking from the Abbey down through the woods, past some cottages which he owned to the locks on the part of the river which had been canalized. We would bait our hooks with pellets of bread, lower them into the river and watch the floats twitching as fish nibbled. But we never, ever, caught one, being there for the sheer pleasure of being with Grandad, wandering along the river bank immersed in its peace and beauty. He used to boast that he had read Izaac Walton's *Compleat Angler* from cover to cover, fished for fifty years and never caught a fish. Probably true.

His fixed routine was reflected in his wardrobe. During the day, at work or playing bowls or croquet, he wore a cream-coloured cotton jacket and the striped dark-grey trousers usually associated with morning dress. If we went out, even if to go fishing, it was a three-piece suit, and in the evenings a brocade smoking jacket with a fez. And always, of course, a gold pocket watch on a chain looping over his ample stomach.

During our stays at Beeleigh we would go on day trips with Granny and Grandad, piling into the large car with Joe Little driving. Often the large Mrs Little, known affectionately as the

Duchess, would take the opportunity to come with us, sitting up front with Joe, looking somehow like a galleon in full sail, while we squeezed in the back. Sometimes it was a shopping trip to Colchester but more usually it was to Southend. Granny would go shopping, Grandad would take us to the Kursaal funfair (we always used the German pronunciation; recently this caused much amusement to new, Essex-born friends who apparently pronounce it 'Curzle'), a wonderland for young children with its rides and steam organs and candyfloss. We'd go from ride to ride, Grandad buying the tickets. Sometimes we were joined by other children, strangers tagging along behind this tubby, silver-haired, genial, latter-day Pied Piper. Our motley procession would stop now and then for us all to go on the rides. He didn't know, neither did he care, who all these children were; he simply counted the heads and paid for the tickets and in doing so added a little to the sum of the world's happiness. A quiet lesson in generosity for us, his privileged grandchildren.

On one of our visits we were joined by a grandson of Granny's guardian Admiral Webb, a boy a couple of years younger than me. Granny bought him new clothes, as she did us. She was effectively repaying his grandfather's generosity to her in her childhood, another quiet lesson in how generosity can cascade down the generations. Fifty years later, just after I joined the board of Foyles, we had a letter from him, acknowledging this.

But the greatest joy of our visits to Beeleigh was being given the complete freedom of his wonderful library. As children it was a place of wonder that William encouraged us to explore and use. We could turn the pages of exquisite illuminated manuscripts, the gold leaf as shiny as the day the scribes applied it. There were books with fore-edge paintings, only revealed when the pages were fanned out. There were books so large we could hardly lift them and books so small they could only be read with a magnifying glass. There was Nelson memorabilia, a snippet of sail from HMS *Victory*, a lock of his hair, some of his letters to Emma Hamilton. There were snuff boxes and card cases and small jewelled caskets. There were medieval musical instruments and bone-handled tablets for teaching the letters of the alphabet – all were housed in that beautiful barrel-roofed room with the pervasive aromas of leather and Havana cigars.

It was a place of inspiration and we allowed ourselves to be inspired. William taught us to love books and beautiful things. I had a privileged upbringing: a great part of that privilege was being allowed, encouraged, to handle beautiful old books. To take out a Third Folio Shakespeare and to be told that it once belonged to Samuel Pepys, to hold a leaf from a Gutenberg bible, to stroke the binding of an Italian fourteenth-century Book of Hours – that's privilege.

After William died, Christina moved in and eventually the doors to the library were locked, the books gathered dust and that link to our youth was severed. When the collection was finally sold after Christina's death, I sat through the three-day auction at Christie's in King Street, watching all those beautiful books, friends from my childhood, being held up, bid for and sold, a library melting away with individual books going to other collections. I consoled myself with the thought that they would become the nuclei of other libraries but I suspect that most were swallowed up by institutions, never again to inspire small children.

*   *   *

Although the business had delivery vans from early on (I have a letter William wrote to Winston Churchill in 1927, offering to buy any surplus books from his library, sending a Foyles buyer who would 'make an immediate offer, pay cash and remove the books in our motor van' - the offer was not taken up), William Foyle himself never drove a car, neither did he own very many. Those he did own were not run-of-the-mill. His first was, I believe, bought in 1926 and usually driven by a chauffeur. It was also on occasion driven by his fourteen-year-old son Dick; Grandad told us that if they saw the police they would quickly change places and Dick would steer from the passenger side while instructing his father what to do with the pedals.

His first limousine was a large, beautiful and opulent 1935 Daimler originally built for a maharajah who changed his cars after a year or so. The driver was partitioned off from the passengers and the interior was all walnut and leather. Between the rear seat and the partition there were three extra seats which folded out so that they faced forward, providing seating in the back for six. By about 1953 the Daimler was becoming unreliable and William decided to replace it with a Rolls-Royce. He went to the Jack Barclay showroom in Berkeley Square in Mayfair to see what was available. Pointing at a Silver Wraith he asked the salesman, in his cockney accent (some of his Hoxton vowel sounds don't transfer easily to the page):

'Aah much is that one?'

'That one, sir, costs £5,000,'

replied the salesman, disdainfully.

'Okay,' said William, *'I'll 'ave it.'*

'We'll require a cash deposit, sir.'

'Naah, I'll bring the £5,000 this afternoon,'

which he did, in cash, in a briefcase, to the surprise of the salesman.

Grandad gave most people nicknames. His wife was never Christina, always Top; she in turn called him Bottom. My mother was Bright Eyes, her sister was Babs, but I don't remember their brother being anything but Dick. His brother and business partner Gilbert was Annie Laurie and my dad was Rocky, both for contrary reasons: Gilbert had a high-pitched, almost shrill voice, Annie Laurie's 'voice was sweet and low'; and Rockefeller had a way with money which my father noticeably lacked. My sisters, Tina, Margaret and Julie and I were respectively Sally, Sarah, Susan and Sammy and to this day there are still some who call my middle sister Sarah.

His generosity had a significant impact on my early life. He bought my parents their house, the house in which I was born, although I never recall him visiting. On moving to Beeleigh Abbey he gave Ilfra Lodge to his son Dick. In 1955 he took my father and my uncle to the London Motor Show and bought them each a car, a Mark 7 Jaguar for my uncle Dick and an Armstrong Siddeley Sapphire for Dad. This was the car in which I eventually practised for my driving test, a substantial vehicle nearly two tons in weight but still capable of 100 mph. William also paid for our family holidays, which during my teens were spent in Switzerland and Italy, and he paid for the education of all six of his grandchildren.

When I was a child Foyles had a carpenter and handyman whose name I never knew, but who made things that were and are still significant to me. Some eighty years ago when my oldest sister was born he made a wooden Noah's Ark, complete with animals in matching pairs, which gave us endless pleasure during our visits to Beeleigh. It has since been played with by my children and grandchildren. He made the stations and other accessories to Grandad's wonderful train set, O-gauge steam-powered Bassett-Lowke locomotives , which ran on brass rails with wooden sleepers round the very large attic at Beeleigh and which I now have and will one day pass on to my grandchildren. And he turned a magnificent but unsafe walnut tree from the Abbey gardens into a beautiful dining suite which my parents used for forty-five years and is now used by one of my sisters.

He was a constant figure throughout my childhood and my teens. A few years before he died he took my mother and me on holiday to Venice, immediately after the Film Festival. With his flowing silver locks and slightly eccentric looks he usually attracted interest and, as we strolled through St Mark's Square, I saw someone point and heard the whispered 'Maestro!' We stayed at the Bauer Grunwald Hotel, rode in a gondola and visited the glass factory on Murano where he bought my mother a chandelier which now hangs in the living room of my oldest sister. He also bought me, from a small shop in St Mark's Square, a silver cigarette case which, although a non-smoker since 1971, I treasure as the only physical gift from him which I still have.

In May 1963 William suffered a stroke and my sisters and I went down to Beeleigh to see him for the last time. By the time we got there Grandad could no longer speak, all those words he so loved unable to find voice. He was sitting up in his big old four-poster bed with Mr Quy, the gardener, sitting behind him, sprawled across the pillows, crying quietly but quite unashamedly, supporting William so he would retain some little dignity. Mary, the cook, a strapping, six-foot-tall, red-haired and freckled Irish lady, was spoon-feeding him. We knew that we would never see him again, never play bowls or croquet or dominoes with him again, never again walk in the sunshine along the banks of the River Chelmer pretending to fish. Two days later, on 4 June 1963, he died.

For as far back as I could remember there had been monthly evensong services at Beeleigh in the summer. Now there was one final service, fittingly William's funeral, held on an appropriately sunny day. Incense, which he had loved, was burning in the censers and the coffin, on which my grandmother had placed a single red rose, seemed too small to contain such a large personality. We sang 'The Holy City (Jerusalem)' and remembered William and shed a tear. He is buried in Highgate Cemetery, along with John Galsworthy, George Eliot, Christina Rossetti, many of Charles Dickens's family and of course Karl Marx.

The last I heard of Mr Quy, who loved my grandfather and who loved Beeleigh's gardens and made them beautiful, was that Christina, who had claimed the house for her own after my grandmother died some years later, had sacked him.

My grandad was a wonderful eccentric and I miss him still. He brought joy into many lives, he introduced books to people from all walks of life through his great, sprawling bookshop of organized chaos, in his time without question the finest in the world. He was kind, fun, witty and extraordinarily generous, childlike, wise and learned. He gave us a love of books and mischief in equal measure and encouraged us to help others and see good in all people. For all his considerable wealth he never lost his common touch or cockney accent, but was still, to me and many others, a maestro. He set an example of generosity, open-mindedness and above all fairness. His life was rich and full of people from all races, religions and classes and I never heard him reference anyone by their background, only as individuals. When you are a child you think that grandads last for ever. Suddenly, you're grown-up and they don't and you're a little more alone in the world.

William and Gilbert had started Foyles on their mother's kitchen table and turnover in the first year was a few hundred pounds. By the time of William's death sixty years later turnover had reached £4m and Foyles accounted for a little over 8% of all book sales in the UK.

My mother inherited, by example rather than genetics, his open-minded fairness and generosity and in her turn set an example to my sisters and me. I remember her brother Dick as a warm, generous fun-loving uncle, a very close friend of both my parent's, sadly to die in 1957, one of the many unrecorded, delayed casualties of the Second World War. But DNA isn't everything and Christina was different.

2. CHRISTINA

CHRISTINA FOYLE, 'AUNTIE CHRISSIE', WAS born in 1911, the second child of William and Christina Foyle and my mother's younger sister. I remember her as beautiful, charming, witty and intelligent. I also remember her as self-centred, ruthless and vindictive. She could be both mean and extraordinarily generous, compassionate and spiteful.

Her very complex personality was heavily influenced by a significant period in her early childhood. At the age of five she contracted tuberculosis and spent some six months in a hospital in Margate. During that time, at the height of the First World War, her parents were unable to visit her. Most of the other patients were wounded service men recovering from the horrors of war, for whom she must have been a reminder of home, of innocence and family. Apparently she used to dance for them; there may have been darker incidents. Certainly, when she returned home she was changed. My mother remembered running to greet her with outstretched arms, welcoming back her beloved little sister, only to be pushed aside and ignored. I suspect that the whole experience coloured her attitude to life in general and men in particular. On her return she turned to the son of a neighbour, Ronald Batty, the same age as herself, who became her constant companion and eventually her husband, her loyal supporter and her best friend for the next seventy-seven years.

Christina and my mother both began working in the family business in 1928, after they returned from a year at finishing school in the little village of Wilderswil, near Interlaken in Switzerland. While my mother remained on the shop floor, working in the music department where she served, among others, Louis Armstrong and Paul Robeson, Christina, Babs as William called her, rapidly became what today would be known as his PA. I do not think she spent much time working on the shop floor but set out to understand the business in its entirety.

William trusted her enough to send her, at the age of twenty-one, to Leningrad, now and previously St Petersburg, to collect bad debts, Russians in the new era of communism being, apparently, notoriously poor payers. Most of the debtors were academics, living in insalubrious areas of the city; she came back with very little money but with a fund of stories of stepping over drunks in dark stairways. Years later she wrote of her trip there in a rather critical article about Russia in the *Sunday Express*. She received a letter from the Soviet Embassy telling her that she would not be welcomed back.

An experience I had many years later suggests that, while Foyles was great at selling books overseas, it was less good at getting paid. In the early 1980s Christina's husband Ron who, in addition to looking after the property portfolio also controlled the finances, heard that I was travelling regularly to Kuwait and asked me if I could collect some old debts from there. He gave me a large brown envelope on which was written 'Kuwait'. It contained a handful of index cards on each of which was written, in pencil, a name and address, a date, the name of a book and an amount. As an accountant I realized that this was Foyles' debtors ledger, at a time when most firms of a similar size had computerized accounting systems.

One particular foreign debt was paid in an unusual way, as we discovered after Christina died. Going through some of her things at Beeleigh I came across a vanity case in crocodile skin with gold fittings. It was empty, apart from a simple visiting card which read 'Juan Peron'. Apparently Eva Peron had ordered some books when Argentina had few foreign reserves and in payment her husband had sent Christina, who shared some of Evita's characteristics, the vanity case.

Perhaps Christina's greatest achievement was her literary luncheons, which arose from a chance remark she made to William in 1930 when she was nineteen. She suggested that it would be nice to give readers a chance to get together with authors and hear them speak. This accorded with the seventh of William's 'Aims as a Bookseller' and, ever one to enable others, he told her to go ahead and set something up. So, in her own words, 'with the optimism of youth, I wrote to the five best-known authors of the day – George Bernard Shaw, H. G. Wells, Barrie, Bennett and Rudyard Kipling – suggesting a date to each of them. Of course they all refused. Wells, in his refusal, added a note that the letters he received from his readers convinced him that he had no desire to meet them in the flesh'.

Christina persevered and, on 21 October 1930 held her first Literary Luncheon, for 200 people, at the Holborn Restaurant with, as guest of honour, Lord Darling, a renowned judge and author. It was a success, so she organized more in the succeeding months. In 1931 the luncheons moved to larger and grander venues, the Dorchester and the Grosvenor House and soon attracted audiences of up to 2,000. More than 700 were held, ten per year until 2005, with the 700th being held as Foyles reached its century in 2003. The list of guests of honour reads like a *Who's Who* of the period, ranging from Emperor Haile Selassie in 1936 to Madeleine Albright in 2002, Kim Philby's father Jack in 1937 to the Soviet Ambassador in 1970, Dylan Thomas in 1953 to Laurie Lee in 1956, Evelyn Waugh in 1934 to Ian Fleming in 1964, and from John Lennon in 1964 to Charlie Chaplin in 1969.

The speakers received no fee and the story of Charlie

Chaplin's attendance illustrates the prestige attaching to the luncheons. Dame Sybil Thorndyke, due to speak at the November 1969 luncheon, broke her leg shortly before. The replacement, the actor Robert Morley, agreed to speak in her place but had to cancel on the morning of the luncheon, being laid low with seasonal illness. Christina had read in the paper that Chaplin was visiting London, she tracked him down at his hotel and asked him, at remarkably short notice, whether he would speak. He immediately accepted.

*   *   *

When in 1937 my mother married, Christina told her that, as Foyles didn't employ married women she had to leave, which she did, settling into the domestic life she wanted and which Christina would have hated. Christina and Ron married the following year, but the same rules apparently didn't apply to her. They were, of course, very different: Winnie, Bright Eyes to her father William, with two younger siblings, was always maternal; Christina, damaged in her own childhood, channelled whatever affection she may have had into her husband and her pets. A couple of years before she died she wrote, in a letter to me: 'I have one dog, eight cats, six peacocks, six tortoises, five hedgehogs, not to mention the chickens, ducks, geese and budgerigars, but having no children I find a lot of pleasure from pets.'

Throughout her time at Foyles Christina relied heavily on Ron and was in turn very protective of him. When the Second World War broke out her younger brother, my uncle Dick, joined the Navy and my father the Army; for Ron, Christina arranged a reserved occupation, a job in a munitions factory, making him ineligible for military service. He was, apparently, the only man doing unskilled work on the factory floor and I can only assume must have been utterly humiliated, but it served Christina's purposes to have him around rather than away fighting in the war. He was by her side all the time she ran Foyles and, coming from a family of North London estate agents, he played a significant part in building up the property portfolio which ensured the survival of the business, insulating it to a degree from the vicissitudes of the book trade.

When in the 1920s Foyles moved from 135 to 113–119 Charing Cross Road it acquired the freehold, paid for out of accumulated profits. From then on surplus profits were invested in property. After the book clubs were set up in the 1930s, with hundreds of thousands of members paying in advance for books which the company bought on ninety days' credit, cash flow was very strong and was partly used to finance the purchase of property. By the late 1960s the property portfolio was such a large part of the overall business that there was a company reorganization and the property was transferred into a separate company, Noved Investment Company (the unusual name being simply Devon spelt backwards – Grandad had loved Devon). This was a least in part motivated by Christina's obsession with privacy: Noved was an unlimited company and therefore was not required to file accounts at Companies House. There were three separate strands to the portfolio: commercial property in and around Charing Cross Road, residential property in North London and Beeleigh Abbey with surrounding agricultural land. By the time of Christina's death Noved was worth many times as much as the bookshop and, as she left the bulk of her substantial estate 'for charitable purposes, Christina's share effectively funded the Foyle Foundation, set up by her executors, which continues to give significant financial support to charities including many promoting literacy.

Although the relationship between Christina and Ron was one of mutual support and affection, there was never any doubt as to who was the boss. I have been told that when they were both working in the shop she would decide it was time to lunch, phone Ron to tell him she was on her way down to the car and if he didn't immediately stop whatever he was doing and meet her there she would go without him. When he died in 1994 he was cremated, his ashes brought back to Beeleigh and left temporarily in the potting room. After some months her housekeeper asked, tactfully, what should be done with them. She gave it some thought and replied that they should be buried in the part of the garden reserved for her much-loved pets. As she generally preferred animals to people this was, in its way, a compliment.

While not known as a great raconteur Christina had a fund of amusing stories. I recall her telling us that once she had been walking down Charing Cross Road with a friend, a peer of the realm and chairman of one of the great industrial conglomerates. An American tourist walking up from Trafalgar Square stopped them to ask the way to Foyles. Christina directed him and said, 'And by the way, I'm Christina Foyle!' 'Well, it's an honour to meet you, ma'am,' he said, impressed. She then introduced her friend: 'And this is Lord Nelson.' The tourist turned and fled.

During the week Christina and Ron lived in a duplex flat accessed through Ron's second-floor office. It had a wood-panelled corner living room, a small kitchen and two bedrooms on its upper floor. As well as being their weekday base the flat was used to entertain visitors. In the winter she kept her tortoises there. On one occasion she was entertaining a well-known lady romantic novelist who picked one of them up and made little cooing noises to encourage it to emerge from its shell; she was told that she was addressing the wrong end. On one of the many occasions that Foyles was in dispute with the Inland Revenue a particularly persistent tax inspector was apparently invited into the flat to discuss the problem informally, plied with copious quantities of sherry and was last seen weaving his way back through the shop gently waving a Union Jack. Grandad had a different approach: for the less welcome visitors he kept in his office a chair which had one leg slightly shorter than the other three, guaranteed to keep the visitor off-guard and distracted.

Another visitor she invited for a drink, this time in her large penthouse, was a young bookseller of whom she had read, Tim Waterstone, who had just opened his first bookshop in the Old Brompton Road. The part of Foyles on the north side of Manette Street, housing paperbacks, history, law and theology, was leasehold. The lease was expiring and she didn't want the hassle of renewing, so she offered it to this smart young man. Tim of course said yes, opened an excellent shop in direct competition with Foyles and went on to build up the most successful chain of bookshops in the UK, exploiting opportunities which perhaps she should have done decades earlier. I spoke to Tim about this some years ago and he told me that not only did she give him a wonderful opportunity, but it took her some time to sort out the utilities, so Foyles paid Waterstone's electricity bills for a couple of years.

The main customer lift in the shop was manually operated, with a control rather like that of a speedboat, forward for down, backward for up. The operator was a delightful lady, Mrs Turner, who had an artificial leg and sat on a high stool in one corner, leaving room for only three customers at a time. The doors were of the old-fashioned concertina grille type, unchanged since the lift had been installed in the 1920s. If any door was opened while the lift was moving, it stopped immediately and the doors were easily forced. One night in the 1950s Christina and Ron heard burglars in the shop below them and Ron, who slept naked, leaped out of bed, grabbed the first garment he could find, the dinner jacket he had been wearing the evening before, left the flat and got in the lift to go down and investigate. The intruders, of course, heard the lift descending. They wrenched open the doors, jamming the lift between floors and fled. Eventually Christina had to summon the fire brigade, who rescued her dinner-jacket-clad but otherwise stark-naked husband. Christina told the story with great amusement; Ron was not amused.

Although William had notionally retired from day-to-day management shortly after the war he had remained as chairman and a powerful presence, retaining his office in Charing Cross Road and his influence over the business for another ten years or so. Christina took over actual control in the early 1950s and it is noticeable that after that there were few innovations. Routine turned to complacency and eventually boredom.

Gradually, as she grew weary of the responsibility of running the family business, neglect crept in. Parts of the business which had been profitable were allowed to die. At some point the travel agency closed down, the philately department disappeared and the crafts department stopped selling raffia. In 1983 John Gifford Ltd ceased publishing and about the same time the Foyles book clubs, which had been such a great cash-generator, quietly stopped sending out their monthly selections. Interestingly in 2017 Foyles set up something on a much small scale but not dissimilar, 'A Year of Books', a scheme whereby customers receive a book a month, chosen by Foyles staff. It has proved popular.

* * *

Christina and I never had a close relationship. There was strong mutual antipathy between my father and her, for reasons which will never be known, and that antipathy was passed on to me.

Nevertheless, I have happy childhood memories of visiting her at her lovely old Tudor home in Essex, de Lâches, in the village of Cold Norton, heavily timbered with wattle-and-daub interior walls, beautifully furnished while remaining cosy, a grand piano which she and Ron both played competently, a warm house which they shared with a well-documented ghost, a house where they both relaxed. Looking back I can see that it must have been quite an ordeal having four small children intruding into their child-free lives. I recall falling into their weed-choked pond and having to wear a pair of Ron's underpants while my own clothes dried and other similar mishaps.

For several years after the war Christina, Ron and my mother went skiing in Arosa, in Switzerland, always staying at the Post Hotel. In 1950 she took my two older sisters, in 1951 it was my turn. We travelled overland, first on the Golden Arrow from Victoria to Dover, the train on which my father had been a waiter some twenty-five years before, then the ferry to Calais, followed by the overnight train to Chur in the east of Switzerland. It was my first trip abroad and I remember waking before dawn in the cabin I shared with my mother and lifting a corner of the blind, seeing my first mountains, which grew increasingly impressive as we travelled through the Jura into the Alps.

We arrived in Chur mid morning and changed to the small two-coach local train to Arosa. The journey should have taken less than two hours, climbing 1,500 metres in its 25 km length. But it snowed and it snowed and it snowed. The first light flurries were falling as we left Chur; the flurries became a snowstorm, the snowstorm became a blizzard. The wheels began to slip and eventually the driver had to stop and ask the passengers to help him clear snow off the line in order for the train to move forward again. We climbed down and took turns to shovel enough snow so the train could get traction and move forward a few yards. These stops became increasingly frequent. At last, at about four o'clock as the light started to fade, we reached a short tunnel, hardly longer than the train, which afforded us shelter from the growing risk of avalanche.

The driver telephoned up to the next village, Litzirüti, to ask for help. Periodically during the late afternoon and evening we were told that snowploughs were on their way, coming up from Chur or down from Arosa, but none of them made it. Eventually, as we were settling in for a hungry night, some skiers came down from Litzirüti with hot chocolate and salami sandwiches. A wartime child, I was unfamiliar with salami; Christina told me it was donkey meat. I ate only the bread and slept hungrier than necessary! She had, as I have said, a mischievous sense of humour.

We woke the next morning, cold and hungry, to find the entrance to the tunnel had been blocked by an avalanche and the accumulation of snow at other end was six feet deep. Some guides managed to ski down from Litzirüti , their ski tracks making a pathway up which we could walk. It was a brilliantly still, cold, sunny day, to me a sunlit fairyland of mountains and snow, but to the guides it was a treacherous, unstable mountainside with snow overhanging everything. We walked in single file, I directly behind a very nervous Ron, Christina, nonchalant throughout, behind me, my mother at the back. With all the excitement of a nine-year-old in a real-life adventure I chattered away. The guide in front said, in a heavy whisper, '*Nicht sprechen!*', which meant nothing to me until Ron turned round and translated: 'Shut! Up!' No doubt it reinforced his belief that children should be seen and not heard, or preferably neither seen nor heard.

As we walked we saw several avalanches on the other side of the valley, beautiful puffs of white tumbling snow followed a few seconds later by a muted rumble, the only indication of their destructive power. After an hour or so we reached Litzirüti where we spent two more nights while snowploughs cleared the line, looking out at the beautiful but impossibly slender suspension bridge which we had to cross at the start of our onward journey. We finally reached Arosa some seventy-two hours late. As no one had been able to leave the town for three days our hotel was still full, so we were initially accommodated elsewhere. The street lights weren't working and those brave enough to venture out did so holding candles. Snow was many feet deep and the candle-lit town almost impossibly beautiful, although I suspect that Christina thought that the inconvenience outweighed the beauty.

It was, incidentally, my first experience of being involved in an event which made the national press. On our return we were shown a report in the *Daily Mail*, according to which, 'The women and children were singing and praying.' No, we weren't;

we were playing 'I Spy', possibly the first and last time Christina Foyle did so. Many people died in the Alps that winter, but to me in was brilliant, my first foreign adventure.

*   *   *

Christina created for herself a safe and pampered world and neither knew nor cared very much about how ordinary people lived. She claimed she couldn't boil an egg and I doubt she ever cooked a meal for herself. I was living in Nairobi in the early 1970s and she stopped over to visit us en route to South Africa, where Foyles had a couple of branches and she had a house. Over dinner I asked how her flight from London had been. 'Very comfortable,' she replied. 'We flew first class.' A pause: 'I don't understand why everyone doesn't fly first class.'

Christina was obsessive about her personal privacy. She obviously considered that the company and the cash it generated was hers and used to write out cheques for her personal expenditure. She would never write on the cheque stubs either the amounts or the payees and the bookkeepers and auditors had to use their imagination, an attribute not usually associated with their profession. Beeleigh Abbey had septic tank drainage: One day there were problems with the tank overflowing and the maintenance people were called in. On opening up the tank they found it was clogged up with old bank statements. Obviously Christina was flushing them down the toilet in the hope that, by destroying bank statements, no one would know what she was spending.

She treated the tills as her own piggy bank, helping herself to whatever she wanted. After her death, bags of cash were found stashed in cupboards at Beeleigh. Her executor showed me a brief-case he was taking to the bank, stuffed full of notes in several different currencies, including a number of the old white £5 notes which had been withdrawn from circulation nearly forty years earlier.

She was a notoriously bad employer, not allowing the staff

39

the most basic of rights. They were not permitted to join trade unions, but in 1965 some of them did so clandestinely. She heard of it and asked one trusted employee to attend a meeting of the union and report back. He duly went to the meeting and disappointed her by reporting that he himself had been persuaded to join. Eventually the union called a strike. Christina simply told Ben Perrick, Foyles marketing manager and the organizing brains behind the Literary Luncheons, to sort it out and flew with her husband to New York where she remained until the strike fizzled out of its own accord.

A question about the strike was asked in Parliament by one of the union-sponsored MPs known for his strident left-wing views. Family folklore has it that Christina was so angry she stuck a pin in a picture of him and he suffered a heart attack shortly afterwards but, like many stories about Christina, I suspect that has been embellished over the years. In the preface to her commonplace book *So Much Wisdom* she refers to the strike, obliquely, as 'vicious onslaughts of wreckers against Foyles'.

Christina's disdain for the staff is shown by the standard letter sent on her instructions to job applicants in the 1980s:

Thank you for your letter.

When you are next in London would you kindly call for an interview any Monday between 4 and 5 p.m. but please do not make a special journey as the fares are so heavy.

Would you kindly bring this letter with you, together with your letter of application, returned herewith.

Yours truly
Personnel manageress

A number of people have recorded that if, at interview, they showed an interest in or knowledge of a particular subject, music perhaps, they were allocated to a completely unrelated department, say, history or politics. A book-trade friend tells the story that, fresh from university and full of ambition, he arrived for interview. He knocked on her office door and entered. Christina stopped what she was doing, looked him up and down, said, 'No, I don't think so' and returned to her paperwork. He left, still unemployed, but went on to a successful career in publishing.

Another friend told me recently of the interview process she went through in the 1970s. She was told to go into an office where Christina was sitting behind a desk, going through papers and signing letters. She waited. Eventually:

'Do you play a musical instrument?'

My friend was puzzled: she was here to be interviewed for a bookselling job.

'Well, do you?' barked Christina.

'Er, yes. The flute,' lied my friend.

Christina continued signing letters. My friend waited.

'Do you like cats?'

Again, my friend was confused.

'Well, do you?' barked Christina again.

'Er, yes.'

'Go and see my secretary. She'll tell you what to do.'
My friend went on to have a very successful career as a bookseller, only the first few months of which were spent in Foyles.

A significant percentage of the people I have met during my years in the book trade started their careers in Foyles and a number tell similar stories. When I returned from living in Africa, even though I was most definitely not interested in a job, Christina assumed I would be asking for one at some stage and told me that on principle she never employed anyone who had been an expatriate as 'they are far too relaxed'.

In March 1990 someone wrote to her, anonymously, to say he or she apparently witnessed two Foyles security guards beating up a suspected shoplifter. As the Staff Rules, drawn up in 1985 and still notionally applicable at the time of her death, stated: 'It is the policy of Foyles to win the highest possible reputation for genuine courtesy – such courtesy as really well-bred people would show to visitors to their own homes,' this obviously upset her. She replied:

Thank you for your letter. I immediately telephoned our manager, but he says that nobody has been stopped for stealing books from Foyles, and we don't have security guards. Possibly, they were people from Waterstones, or one of the many other bookshops, or maybe it was just some Soho violence, or the Mafia even. Anyway, I am very sorry that you were upset by the scene.

I am pretty well sure that none of our staff were involved, because people who work in bookshops are usually rather frail and avoid any kind of violence.

As sales began to decline in the 1970s Christina gradually reduced the number of sales staff, which may have saved money in the short term but contributed to the downhill spiral of the business. Having little rapport with the staff she did not trust them to handle cash and introduced the system whereby the customer would first find their books, then get a member of the sales staff to write out a chit which the customer took to one of the cashiers' booths for payment. The chit was stamped and taken back to the sales person, who would hand over the books. During busy periods this involved queuing three times, to get the chit, to pay and to claim the books, a system eloquently described by Wendy Cope:

Yes, I remember Foyles – too well –
Because, one Saturday in June,
I went to buy some books and stood
The whole confounded afternoon
In queues – to have the volumes put
Inside a paper bag and then
A stretch at the cashier's desk.
I saw that people queued again
To claim them from the foreign boy
Who served the customers or would
Have done, if he could speak the language.
No! I thought. Why ever should
I spend good money here? And left,
Bookless, my education spoiled.
I would have read all Gibbon's work
By now. I tried, but I was foyled.

This poem was written as an entry for a *New Statesman* competition in 1980. Readers were asked to contribute a poem about waiting. Later I learned that the magazine had asked a lawyer to take a look at the poem, in case it was libellous. He cleared it for publication on the grounds that it was true.

Christina also thought it a waste of the time of the diminishing number of sales staff to handle telephone enquiries, so anyone calling the company's number heard a recorded announcement giving the shop opening times and no invitation to leave a message.

Christina and Ron shunned modern technology. Apparently in one interview when asked about such developments Ron replied, 'We have no need for computational machines'. A few years before Christina died the manager, unknown to them, bought a small computer and used it for sales analysis. On her weekly visits she was always given a handwritten summary of the previous week's sales and after the clandestine purchase a new staff member, unaware of her dislike of machines, presented her with a printout of the sales figures 'straight off the computer'. 'The computer? Get rid of it!'

* * *

By the time of my grandmother's death in 1977 Christina had moved into Beeleigh Abbey and become totally proprietorial towards it and its contents, although through the complexities of the companies and my grandfather's will she only had beneficial ownership of some two-thirds of the house and one-third of the very valuable library. She made a derisory offer to buy out the other shareholders' interests in the library. I advised my mother not to accept and to call a meeting of the beneficiaries to decide on the fairest way to sort out the complex structure. As my mother was the oldest of her generation we insisted that the meeting should be at her house at Burnham-on-Crouch, a dozen miles from Beeleigh.

It must have been one of the few times Christina ever attended a meeting at a place not of her choosing, but she and Ron came, as did my two cousins, the sons of her late brother Dick. I chaired the meeting and she reluctantly agreed to have a professional valuation of the library. The valuation was very significantly higher than the figure Christina had proposed and my mother's eventual settlement was three times greater than her original offer. Christina never forgave me for that.

Under the terms of the settlement, William Foyle's grandchildren were each entitled to take a few things from Beeleigh Abbey, mementos of happy times in our childhood. We duly made our choices and I, having the largest vehicle, a Volvo Estate, was delegated by my sisters to collect them. Christina's version of this episode, which she spread round the family, was that I arrived in a pantechnicon to take away her things and, as I learnt years later, from then on she referred to me as 'Burglar Bill'.

For more than sixty years Christina's right-hand man was Ben Perrick. He was two years older than Christina and survived her by a month. I had known him all my life and sometime in the mid 1990s I bumped into him in the King's Road, alighting from a bus I was about to board. We had a chat and went our separate ways. Much later one of the long-serving staff, Kay Whalley, always happy to share gossip about Christina, told me that on his return to the shop he mentioned to Christina that he had bumped into me. 'I hope you didn't speak to him,' she said, familial affection not being her strong suit.

Some years before she died I visited her at Beeleigh. We discussed family: I asked her about William's mother, of whom I know little. She said the past was of no interest to her, what was interesting was the future. The conversation moved on to Foyles and chatting to her I sensed a weariness with the business. She had had a very comfortable life, living in a beautiful house in lovely countryside and spoke of the business as if it had become a burden. I had recently left full-time work and tentatively offered to buy her shares in the business. She laughed, told me that she regularly had offers to buy but would never contemplate selling. I was then given her usual polite, genteel dismissal: 'Would you like to look around the garden?' I realized then that she looked upon the business as her baby, her creation and she intended to die while still in control. I think it is possible that, when she eventually chose to die, she did so because she confidently believed that the business was, finally, beyond any hope of survival and her baby would die with her.

After Ron died she hardly visited the shop, living on her own at Beeleigh, looked after by a handful of staff. She had by then fifteen cats, several tortoises, a noisy gaggle of peacocks and a particularly vicious dog, which bit more or less indiscriminately but had a particular and, in her opinion

45

commendable, taste for accountants and lawyers – she was quoted in *The Bookseller* in 1994 as saying, 'I don't think I've ever found accountants attractive' (I am, incidentally, an accountant but I think her dislike of me had deeper roots). Years later I met a retired lawyer who told me she had worked for the company's solicitors and one of her tasks was to sort out the legal actions arising from the dog's dislikes.

Christina discouraged visitors, but a few days before she died I drove out to see her with my middle sister, probably the only member of the family with whom she was close and to whom she would, occasionally, listen. She had by then more or less stopped eating and even my sister's formidable powers of persuasion were ineffective in changing her mind. I didn't show myself as I thought that might upset her, but I watched her through the gap between the door and its frame, sitting up in her four-poster bed, still elegant, with strong traces of her former beauty, but obviously tired and, from what I could hear of the conversation, tired of living. She had lived an extraordinary life and wasn't going to waste her final days reminiscing about it. The conversation was all about her pets, many of which remained in her room with her until she died a few days later.

When the contents of her will were made public, among her very few legacies was the sum of £100,000 to her then gardener, specifically so he could carry on looking after her dog. He had had the animal put down the day after she died, but still received the money. He was also the prime suspect in a major burglary of her house in Cold Norton years before, when all her furniture and paintings, including a valuable Stubbs and a couple by Alfred Munnings who had been a personal friend, were removed overnight and driven away in a large removal van. She also left £100,000 to a previous general manager of Foyles, who we later discovered had participated in some of the frauds through which several million pounds was stolen from the business. She was not a great judge of people. We recovered the latter legacy through a lengthy legal process.

A couple of days after she died, sitting in my office at my home in Blackmoor I listened to her obituary on the Radio 4 *PM* programme. I don't think in her lifetime she cared much about her legacy, but I thought: what a life! In spite of the animosity that had been between us at times I have great admiration for her. In pure business terms she did nothing to improve Foyles, rather she oversaw its steady decline, but nearly twenty years after her death I still meet people who retain vivid memories of her. She left a great impression on most people she met, but sadly she had turned the wonderful shop passed on to her by her father into the object of affectionate ridicule.

3. THE SHOP

IN THE 1920S WILLIAM WROTE: 'I consider Charing Cross Road the worst architecturally and morally in the world, but it has a wonderful fascination. At night one sees every type of person and every nationality strolling along. It was the site of our shop that Dickens chose as the background to *A Tale of Two Cities*. Soho round the corner has two characters: innocent by day, villainous by night. Houses that look respectable by day open their doors at night to the most sinister interiors. People one meets there lead double lives.' But very early on he had moved his business to Charing Cross Road because for almost a century it had been the heart of London's bookselling.

The Shop had its own personality and influence and belongs in the cast of characters of this memoir. It occupied nearly half an acre of land between Charing Cross Road and Greek Street, an agglomeration of five buildings dating from the eighteenth to the twentieth centuries, with unmatched facades and uneven floor levels. It was on the west side of Charing Cross Road, running north from the old St Martin's School of Art building, turning the corner and continuing along the south side of Manette Street as far as the Pillars of Hercules pub. When William bought it, the property adjacent to the south had not yet become the home of Central Saint Martins College of Art, it

49

was the stables of Crosse & Blackwell's pickle factory across the road – the carthorse still played an important part in urban life.

The centre of the building, 119 Charing Cross Road, was until the 1920s the Rose and Crown pub, named not for some heraldic design but for the two streets on whose corner it stood, Charing Cross Road having been, until the mid nineteenth century, Crown Street, with Rose Street changing to Manette Street to commemorate the hero of Dickens's *Tale of Two Cities* around the same time. In the 1920s the Rose and Crown became Peccorini's wine bar, the owners of which became lifelong friends of my family. My mother always spoke fondly of their son Victor and I suspect he was an early suitor. The basement, used for storage from the 1960s onwards by the medical department, still had a lingering aroma of wine which, occasionally, overrode the less appealing smells coming up from the Victorian drains which ran under the building.

One of the buildings comprising the Shop had a brief flirtation with fame, as I discovered some years ago while sitting in a café in Copenhagen waiting to meet my brother-in-law. Having nothing to read I was looking at one of the prints on the wall, in the slightly unfocussed way one does when passing the time and trying to avoid eye contact with strangers, when I thought 'hang on a minute, that's my office', as the words resolved themselves into '113 Charing Cross Road'. It was a painting by Toulouse Lautrec, an advert he was commissioned to do in 1894 for the confetti factory set up by paper-makers J & E Bella and housed for some years in one of our buildings.

Inside, the Shop was a rabbit warren, rambling between high shelves filled with a mix of new and second-hand books, four million of them when I was a child, and straddled Manette Street. There were still well over a million books at the time of Christina's death, stacked fairly haphazardly on several miles of shelving with the overflow in piles on the floor. There were five sales floors covering more than 40,000 square feet, with a central core housing the aging lift, unchanged since the 1920s, ferrying, very slowly, a few customers at a time between floors. There was also a small assortment of escalators which had been added on Christina's whims with no obvious strategy for giving customers better access to the stock. Towards the end of Christina's reign the layout had become increasingly illogical and the shelving disorderly, adding to the frustration of the paying customers.

The fact that there were multiple unguarded entrances made it attractive to non-paying customers, shoplifters, so at least one section of the public liked the place. The medical department, where average transaction values were exceptionally high, was in the basement, which of course was renamed Lower Ground Floor, a change which fooled no one – it was a claustrophobic space not made any more attractive by its troublesome and malodorous drains. Sometime in the past Christina had installed one of her escalators, which took customers back up from the department to the ground floor where it emerged immediately opposite one of the several street entrances, an ideal rapid escape route for shoplifters. When it became obvious that this had been a poor idea its direction of travel was reversed, simply taking customers down one level.

There was an antiquarian department, a lovely space with wood-panelled alcoves and chandeliers; a music department with turntables and headphones; a travel agency through which in 1959 I booked a two-week skiing holiday in Kitzbuhel; and a philately department selling the stamps which came in on the thousands of letters received every day. There was a gallery, originally on the fourth floor but during Christina's time moved to the second as a separate and rather soulless room off the Art department. In the 1930s the administration offices were part of the second floor and extended into 111 Charing Cross Road, Crosse & Blackwell's horses having become victims of the rise of motor transport.

At the back was a large goods yard to take deliveries of the several tons of books which were processed through the shop every day and of course to house William's and Christina's cars. Off the yard was the carpenter's workshop, where he made and repaired the wooden shelving, of which there was more than thirty miles.

By the time I was born the Shop had a total of some 350 staff, serving hundreds of thousands of customers who came from all over the world. During the Blitz it narrowly escaped a direct hit. We have photos of a bomb crater in Charing Cross Road, spanned by a hastily erected Bailey bridge which William formally named The Foyle Bridge, erected to restore customers' access to the Shop.

It was a place in which a child could happily get lost, lost in time and books, a place of dreams and discovery. My sisters and I visited regularly from the end of the war and throughout our childhood. During the periods when we lived abroad the Shop was one of our first ports of call on visits home and it continued to delight us until it was relocated to its new home.

Now the Shop has gone, demolished to make way for a 300,000-square-foot development of small offices, shops and restaurants. From Foyles' new premises at 107 Charing Cross Road I have looked out at the enormous hole where it used to be. The flippant me thought it looked as if a giant tooth has been removed from the jaw of Soho. The emotional me saw it as an achingly sad and empty space and I felt as I did whenever I saw Grandad's empty chair after he died.

In its heyday the old Foyles building dominated Charing Cross Road like a stately duchess. By the time Christina died it had become the batty old maiden aunt, viewed with a mixture of affection, pity and derision, overtaken by the scarlet lady of Borders across the road and the bluestocking of Blackwells further down. But Foyles was not to be written off. The lovely new building is completely different but developing its own style and appealing to its own fans, the last major Charing Cross Road bookshop standing, neither stately nor batty, but elegant and youthful, ready to meet the challenges of the twenty-first century.

4. FRIDAYS AT THE SHOP

COMING HOME FROM THE WAR in 1946 my father was not invited by Christina to return to Foyles, which he had left when he joined the army in 1940, so he set up a small printing business, in Flitcroft Street, just off the end of Denmark Street. It was less than a hundred yards from the Shop and my mother worked there part-time. I found out much later that it was effectively subsidized by work from Foyles, arranged, unknown to Christina, by William with Ben Perrick, always a good friend to my mother, acting as go-between.

The business had a small van and employed a driver, Mr Watson, who lived a mile or so from us a little to the north of Reigate, in Surrey. Mr Watson, whose first name we never knew, spoke with a soft Surrey accent which, with the spread of suburbia, is probably now extinct. He and his wife occasionally looked after our house and our pets when we went on holiday. The pets included an Indian mynah bird, Simon, like most mynahs a great mimic. I recall that on returning from one such absence the bird's cheerful greeting of 'Good morning Simon' had become, as closely as I can transliterate it, 'Maar'n Soimon'.

During our school holidays we would go to London every Friday, to coincide with Grandad's weekly visit to the Shop. We'd drive up with Dad, or more often be driven up by Mr

Watson in the back of the little van, and be dropped at the printing business. In the basement we would watch and marvel at the alchemy of lumps of lead, for all the world like oversized Cadbury's chocolate bars, being fed into the Linotype machines and metamorphosing into lines and pages of type. These would be fed into the Heidelberg printing presses with their waving arms like bizarre giant mechanical insects, where they would be used to put words on the printed page. But for all the fascination of printing the lure of finished books was greater and we would soon make our way over to the Shop.

At that time Christina had her flat within the shop, a duplex on the second and third floor. It was her sanctuary and was guarded by her husband, the entrance being through his office. Her housekeeper, Mrs Jacques, would keep us supplied with milk and sweets, entertain us with conjuring tricks, tell us stories, sing to and with us and generally keep us out of Christina's hair. Christina tolerated us but never particularly liked children, preferring animals, which Mrs Jacques also looked after. There was a large, exuberant chocolate-brown poodle called Oscar, a Siamese cat and usually a tortoise. One of her duties was to take Oscar for his daily walk and it was a common sight in Soho, which still had many village characteristics including fresh food shops, to see this tall, spindly woman being dragged into butchers' shops where Oscar would grab whatever he could. Christina used to settle up with them monthly, as much later she used to pay compensation to those accountants and tax inspectors bitten by her last dog.

With the flat as our base we would make forays into Soho, or go to the Jacey News Theatre just down Charing Cross Road to watch the morning cartoon programmes. As I write this, seventy years later and knowing Soho well, it seems unthinkable that four small children (we are separated by only six years) should walk together as a little pack, with no adult to protect us, through the heart of Soho. I'm not naive enough to think that the world was a safer place, but possibly today's children

54

are protected to an extent that they lose their natural instinct of self-preservation and the confidence that goes with it.

At noon we would gather for the highlight of the day, lunch at 'The Troc', the old Trocadero restaurant, long gone, replaced by a sad development of a cinema, rather tacky tourist shops and 'entertainments'. The Trocadero then was a sprawling subterranean restaurant at the Piccadilly end of Shaftesbury Avenue. Opened towards the end of the nineteenth century as the flagship of the J. Lyons catering empire, it still thrived in the austerity of the 1950s, although its days were numbered. It offered a limited menu of well-prepared and presented food at middle-market prices to its clientele of businessmen with comparatively modest expense accounts. It was a fat L-shape, a large rectangle with a substantial corner cut out for the kitchens, seating several hundred diners, and as in Lyons Corner Houses they were efficiently served by a substantial number of staff. At one end there was the band, directed by its conductor in his white tie and tails, his flamboyance at odds with the anodyne background music which they played.

These lunches were a family ritual, very precious to us all. Every Friday, any Foyle family members who were in London would turn up. I can't remember my father ever being there; he and Christina had a very active dislike of each other and I think my grandfather's obvious success fuelled my father's sense of inadequacy. It was a family ritual that simply excluded my father, although it included Christina's husband Ron and my uncle Dick's wife Alice. We would have drinks in the bar upstairs, Britvic fruit juices for us children, for most of the adults champagne cocktails in those wide shallow glasses, supposedly modelled on Marie Antoinette's breasts, in which the British at the time served champagne; Alice's preference was for Campari and soda and Ron's a dry martini.

When ready we would descend to the restaurant proper by the imposing staircase which swept down to the top of the L. At a signal from Mr Woods, the maitre d', the band would strike up 'The Happy Wanderer', Grandad's favourite song, and our little procession would wind its way through the lunchers to our reserved table far down on the left-hand side. Grandad, with his flowing silver locks, would lead the way and I remember the pride I felt as a little boy to be associated with such a great and kind and lovable and loved man. We always had the same waiters, directed by Mr Woods, always ready to be the butt of Grandad's jokes, always falling for the electric shock handshake or the bread roll slipped into his pocket.

Although usually just family, Grandad or Christina sometimes invited others, a random selection of friends and acquaintances. I remember once we were joined by the then Bishop of London, who when asked how he should be addressed said 'call me Bish'. On another occasion William invited an American academic who had written a small book of shortcuts in mental arithmetic, which had caught his attention. In addition to his love of books he had a love of figures and as a boy I had watched him run his eyes just once down a column of pounds, shillings and pence and insert the total. I had inherited his love of mental arithmetic and was duly given a copy of the book.

It was at the Troc I was introduced to curry, at a time when Indian restaurants were considered exotic. It was served by an impressively turbaned Indian gentleman, from a trolley with copper domes over the three dishes, mild, medium and hot, the latter, as soon we discovered, to be treated with great caution. We were offered a range of accompaniments, chutneys, poppadoms and the pungent, fishy-flavoured Bombay duck, which now seems unavailable. It was there that I first tasted smoked salmon, at that time an expensive luxury, experienced the theatre of crêpes Suzette and first tried Châteauneuf-du-Pape, Grandad's favourite wine. While we all enjoyed his generosity Grandad would sit at the head of the table, cocooned within his deafness and not participating too much in the conversation, quietly content to be surrounded by his family.

After lunch we would return to the Shop and spend a couple of hours wandering the many departments, lost in the magic of books, gathering up any which took our fancy. The seeds of my passion for books were planted during those childhood afternoons, lost among the miles of shelving, entranced by the range available, books which fed my curiosity, my wanderlust and, as I confessed to my sisters very recently, my pre-adolescent prurience – I had discovered that if I browsed, discretely, the photography department I could occasionally find a photo of a naked lady.

When it was time to be taken home we would stagger into Grandad's office, arms laden with our selections, and ask if we could have them; invariably the answer was 'yes'. To have, as young children, unlimited access to books was a huge privilege, instilling in us a love of reading which continues to this day. I still get a thrill walking around the new Foyles building in Charing Cross Road, to see the range available and to have my eye caught by a book I never knew existed but which cries out for my attention. I still buy more books than I can read. Some demand to be read immediately, others sit on my shelves maturing quietly like good wine, occasionally, also like good wine, to be taken out and enjoyed when the mood or the moment is right.

When I was a teenager Grandad told me I could use his account at the Troc, which I only did a couple of times, to entertain school friends when money, as usual was tight; on one such occasion, as we enjoyed William's largesse and ordered wines we couldn't normally afford, Christina and Ron arrived. They were less than pleased to see me. But she, selectively generous, allowed my sisters, who on occasion stayed at her flat when she was away, to use her account at various Soho restaurants.

Years later, some months after Grandad died, some of us went back to the Troc on a Friday to try to maintain the tradition. Mr Woods was still there. In his will Grandad had left him £100, equal to several weeks' salary. Subdued, he showed us to the old table, served us with his usual dignity and didn't try to hide the tears trickling down his face. We never went back as a family.

5. ME

I WAS BORN IN APRIL 1941, at our home in the outer suburbs in Surrey, to a soundtrack of air-raid-warning sirens, the rumble of heavy bombers and the occasional distant explosion of German bombs. My father had enlisted in the Army and wasn't present and I suspect that had he been there he would have been even less use than the midwife who dived under my mother's bed whenever the sirens went, telling Mum to wait until the doctor arrived. When waiting was no longer an option I slithered into the world unaided.

Home was on a road of fairly modest semi-detached houses some twenty miles south of London which Grandad had bought for my parents a couple of years earlier. Our long narrow garden was mainly given over to vegetables and chickens to supplement our wartime rations. The garden backed onto a strip of woodland, then many hundreds of acres of gorse and bracken-covered common land, which became an adventure playground for me and my three sisters, two older and one younger.

I was five years old when I first remembered meeting my father. As my youngest sister had been conceived when I was two and a half and he was on leave from the army prior to being sent to North Africa, I must have met him but have no memory of doing so. When the war ended he was in Alexandria. He was then posted to Palestine and was still there, in Jerusalem, when the King David Hotel was bombed a year later. By the time he finally left the Army our household had become a tight, bonded, fatherless unit. My mother was the competent head of the household, my sisters were already starting to show the strengths which would carry them through their varied and successful lives and I was the only male.

We knew we had a father but he hadn't figured in our lives for five years. On the day he was to return we went to the top of Vernon Walk, the cul-de-sac in which we lived, eagerly peering into each of the few cars turning into the road. After what seemed like hours with no sign of a father we gave up and walked the hundred yards or so home, entered the house and there he was, a complete stranger, as uncomfortable with us as we were with him. He had brought gifts, things we had read of but never seen because of wartime shortages: a balloon and some bananas. Strange to think now that these were, to small children, things of wonder.

Like so many men of his generation he was an unrecorded casualty of war, having effectively lost the opportunity to be part of his family. I have many fond memories of him, he was a brilliant raconteur, one of the funniest men I have known, but none of those memories involved any physical contact more than a handshake, never a hug or a kiss. Dad was seven when his own father had died in the flu epidemic of 1919 and he was largely brought up by his older sister. My mother loved him till the day he died in 1984, aged seventy-two, from lung cancer and cirrhosis of the liver, his slow self-inflicted death ending a life of unfulfilled potential.

Books have figured large in my life from early childhood onwards. They ignited both my curiosity and my wanderlust. Like most of my generation I started with Enid Blyton and *Swallows and Amazons*, but the book that most changed my life was probably the unlikely *Wings over the Zambezi* by Wilfrid Robertson, which I found in my school library. A less-than-brilliant wartime thriller set in Southern Africa, with the English goodies and German baddies typical of the writing of the time, it fired in my curious ten-year-old self a desire to see Africa, to experience parts of the world which were radically different from the comfortable Home Counties where I grew up. That desire was reinforced by Rider Haggard, G. A. Henty and others. Eventually I was to spend nine wonderful years in East Africa, from my mid twenties to my mid thirties when my enthusiasm and energy were at their peak. I left a piece of my heart there and I return to tend it whenever I can. I moved back to the UK more than forty years ago but to this day when I disembark a plane in Nairobi and smell the red earth and see the smiling faces and hear the laughter a small voice inside me says: 'we're home'.

I went to single-sex boarding schools from the age of seven until I was eighteen, so my life swung between mostly male company during the term time and strong female company in the school holidays. This was a useful grounding for when, very many years later, my career swung from the single-minded male-dominated world of investment banking to the more nuanced book trade, peopled by as many influential women as men.

Thanks to my grandfather's generosity I went to a 'good school' and being reasonably academic I was, in the opinion of the school, Oxbridge material. Unfortunately Oxbridge thought otherwise. No one had told me that other universities were an option so, branded a failure at eighteen, I became a chartered accountant, a profession which taught me much about business and eventually led to a life of travel.

I married young, aged twenty-three, and was a father at twenty-four. My first wife was Danish and shortly after I qualified we moved to Denmark where I worked for Price Waterhouse, forerunner to PWC and at the time the finest accounting firm in the world. After two years I was ready to move on but at twenty-six not ready to return to London. I decided to fulfil my dream of living in Africa and took a two year contract with a Nairobi-based accounting firm affiliated to Deloitte.

Living in Denmark had not been 'exotic'. It was the home of my in-laws, I had been visiting for several years and spoke the language tolerably well. Africa however was an adventure and as all good adventures should, it began with complications. At the time, before the advent of cheap air travel, the usual way to travel intercontinentally was by ship. We were booked on the Union Castle line sailing from London to Mombasa in mid July 1967, but the Six Day War of the previous month had left the Suez Canal blocked. Plans were changed and we flew from Heathrow, in a BOAC VC10, my wife, my twenty-month-old daughter and I, on 20 July 1967. With the aftermath of war in the Middle East and a civil war in Nigeria, flying over North Africa was considered unsafe and the flight was routed via Teheran, where we stopped for refuelling at six in the morning. Determined to sample the mysterious Orient, I went into the terminal and ordered a coffee, expecting some exotic Eastern brew. I received a cup of hot water and a sachet of Nescafé.

We landed at Nairobi's Embakasi airport around midday and were met by one of the partners of the accounting firm I was joining, whose father had started the partnership in 1908. He drove us into Nairobi in his Peugeot 404, past the Nairobi Game Park. I saw an ostrich silhouetted among the thorn trees just inside the fence, my first experience of African wildlife. Perhaps one of the Big Five would have been more exciting but for me the rather comical ostrich did just fine.

* * *

I cannot adequately express the excitement of 1960s Kenya, the vibrancy of a young, developing, multicultural nation. I have never, before or since, felt so completely at home, so much as if I belonged, as I did there. We lived there for nine years. We had our second daughter there, we enjoyed a magical life in the sunshine, we devoted that period of our lives to Africa and Africa gave us much in return. We played, we grew, we made friends, we had fun. Memories crowd together, nine years which can condense into a few sentences or expand to fill books: camping trips with my father-in-law, to Amboseli and Tsavo and Meru, bathing at Buffalo Springs and watching the elephants splashing around where a few minutes before we had been swimming; a weekend with my family camping beside a river in the Samburu Game Reserve, a river which we later found was home to many crocodiles, log fire burning high, pop music of the time playing on our primitive cassette player as we danced and drank wine under a full African moon; sitting with friends on the beach at Kikambala, smoking pot and eating roast chicken, watching the moon climb up from the sea, describe a small arc and set again; watching the sunrise from the top of Kilimanjaro, all of Africa spread beneath me; diving on the reefs of the Indian Ocean.

My working life had its share of variety. I was told on day one that, in addition to audit work for the Nairobi office, I was to spend one week each month supervising two small offices in northern Tanzania, in the towns of Arusha and Moshi. On my first trip there I found out why. The local partner, a Scot, was a difficult alcoholic no longer on speaking terms with the Nairobi partners and I had to mediate between them. Not easy, but the wonderful five-hour drive on dirt roads, dodging giraffe and zebra, having a beer at the end of the day, the only European in a bar in the shadow of Kilimanjaro, and the general joyful unpredictability of Africa, made it worthwhile. Audit work is often thought to be boring, but when the audit clients include remote agricultural estates best reached by light plane, the Serengeti Research Institute on the plains of northern Tanzania where the scientists and their wives dressed for dinner at least once a week, and the Madagascar Hilton built, against local advice, on an old Malagasy graveyard, with its resident ghost on the sixth floor, boring isn't the first word coming to mind.

At the end of my two-year contract I turned down the offer of a partnership because I was not ready to commit to a lifetime in the accounting profession. I became freelance, was involved in an advertising agency and in tourism development, bought into a small country club on the shores of the beautiful Lake Naivasha, negotiated an ambitious Holiday Inn franchise for Africa and the Middle East and arranged the renovation of the Grand Hotel in Khartoum. The Holiday Inn franchise eventually came to nothing, not least because the large white men sent out from Memphis Tennessee tended to lose patience with the African civil servants from our partners, the Kenya Tourist Development Corporation, and 'Cain't you niggrahs get ainythang right?' isn't exactly a winner in black Africa.

Eventually, after nine wonderful years, with daughters of ten and eight needing to have access to better schools than were available in Nairobi at the time, we returned to England. To my surprise I found my motherland was not desperate for someone with my skills and experience, so once more I started venturing abroad and for the next twenty-five years I was living in Surrey but earning a living overseas, mainly in the Gulf, Africa and the Caribbean.

Looking back on my career I can see no obvious reasons for some things to have taken the course they did, but as someone said, 'Life is what happens when you are planning something else.' I probably inherited some of the Foyle entrepreneurship but constrained as it was by my inner accountant I seemed to miss out on the conventional entrepreneur's career path. Fortunately I also inherited a natural optimism and curiosity, with a willingness to accept a challenge. How otherwise would I have been, after leaving Africa, a housebuilder in Portugal, an investment banker in Bahrain, Director of Tourism and Superintendent of Offshore Finance in a small Caribbean nation, Commercial Adviser to the Government of St Helena and, without any sporting ability whatsoever, a participant in the opening ceremony of the 2002 Commonwealth Games?

I have been asked many times if, when young, I wanted to work in Foyles and the answer has always been 'No, why would I?' Although I loved the Shop and books generally, I wanted to plot my own path through life, have my own adventures, carve out my own niches. My mother, as the daughter of a bookseller, was an avid reader and introduced me to books at a very early age. My father left school at fourteen and simply didn't read books. His reading was mainly *Sporting Life* and the racing pages of the daily newspapers. Fortunately I had my sisters as fellow book-lovers and thanks to our mother books were always present in our childhood.

It is always a mystery to me that half of the population never read a book and much of the other half wouldn't be without one. Those of us who read books cannot understand those who don't and vice versa. A year or so after I joined Foyles I was invited to a dinner hosted by our auditors, who had many book-trade clients. I was at a table of ten, with several publishers and a couple of successful authors. Sitting next to me was one of the partners of the audit firm and to fill a rare gap in the conversation he said, to the table in general, 'I never read books myself. What is it you actually like about them?', a comment met by a stunned silence. Those of us who love books cannot pass a bookshop without going in; yet years later I sat for half an hour watching the entrance of our lovely new shop in Birmingham, with its enticing windows, noticing that at least three-quarters of the passers-by didn't spare it a glance. One of life's mysteries.

Coming from a business family, my mother being a Foyle and my father having his own printing business which he set up after the war, business has always fascinated me. I can't take credit for the first business venture in which I was involved – that goes to my two older sisters but at the age of six I was an active partner. We went around our neighbours' gardens collecting rose petals, from which we made rose-water to sell back to the same neighbours. Fortunately my memories from more than seventy years ago are cloudy but I expect they humoured us – we had nice neighbours. I started my own first business venture at school when I was twelve: it was a lending library of comics, of which I had a reasonable collection. As actual cash was rare among my schoolfriends I charged one sweet for a day's comic rental, using some of the sweets to acquire more comics. By the end of term I had a considerably larger collection of rather tatty comics and had learnt a useful lesson for a small boy: while cash may not be king it certainly beats bags of useless, sticky, suppurating sweets. I've owned or managed a number of businesses since, including an advertising agency in Nairobi, a construction company in Portugal and an accountancy practice in Surrey. They had varying degrees of success but were always fun and taught me much about commerce.

Of the various careers I have had and jobs I have done, the most remunerative and least rewarding was investment banking in Bahrain. I was proud of my association with the company, which was itself hugely successful and with which I had had an involvement since the founder, at the time head of Chase Manhattan Bank in the Gulf, asked my advice on the optimum corporate structure for his ambitious plans. But my role was in essence to make extremely rich people even richer, without adding anything of real value. This was brought home to me one day in 1989 when I was in my office in Bahrain. I had a call from a colleague in New York:

'Hey Bill, we've got a great deal. There's this company, we can get it for $100m, $5m equity, $95m debt, two years turning it around, projected IRR 155%!'

'Sounds good, Oliver. What does the company do?'

A pause:

'Is that relevant?'

As it happens the company made fire hydrants, of themselves very useful, but to the investment banker the purpose of buying the company was not to make more or better fire hydrants but to make money from buying and then selling the company.

The investment bank eventually recognized what I could have told them years earlier, that I was not a corporate person and my very remunerative banking career came to an abrupt and unplanned end. This forced me to look for paid employment and eventually after much networking I joined a team of consultants to carry out a strategic review of the economy of a small British Overseas Territory in the Caribbean, the Turks and Caicos Islands. From one of the lowest points of my working and financial life I found myself being tolerably well paid to spend a couple of months in paradise.

* * *

The Caribbean has given me some of my favourite memories. I was chairing a large workshop on the island of Providenciales in TCI, with all the local Government ministers occupying the front row, the chief minister in the centre. He was a Caribbean politician straight out of central casting and, as I was to find out much later when he was my boss and his mistress my subordinate, a thoroughly unpleasant man. He had on the regulation impenetrable dark glasses and was wearing a particularly garish mustard-yellow and lime-green checked suit. Towards the end of a very long day I was taking written questions passed up from the floor and handed to me by one of my colleagues. I unfolded one slip and read, 'You must get the name of his tailor!'

Trying to keep a straight face I rapidly moved on to a real question. Next to him was another minister, Big Louie, a great mass of curly black hair and beard, shirt open to his waist, gold medallion perched on his substantial stomach, a children's picture-book image of a pirate. As I was wrapping up what had to my surprise been a very productive session I asked for one last question. 'I gotta question,' growled Big Louie. 'You wanna job?' The following year I was invited back to set up a tourist board and be Director of Tourism.

My task was to turn a very inefficient Tourist Office into a fully fledged Tourist Board and on the first day I met with the minister of tourism who was also the chief minister, him of the garish suit, not the brightest of politicians. I asked him what his vision for tourism in the islands was. 'We've got the greatest beaches in the world and I want as many people as possible to enjoy them before they get ruined.' I then found out that the lady who had been running the Tourist Office, who was to be my deputy, had been using the office to fund her personal shopping trips to Miami and New York and was the chief minister's mistress. I knew I was going to have an uphill struggle.

This memoir isn't the place to catalogue the fun that struggle afforded me, but my experience with the airlines will give a flavour of it. One of the many problems which the Islands' embryonic tourism industry faced was its restricted air access, the only flights in and out being thrice-weekly Pan Am flights from Miami. Pan Am was known to be struggling to survive and had it stopped operating with TCI having no alternative carrier it would have been disastrous for the islands, so I contacted a number of other carriers and eventually persuaded Cayman Airways to put on an alternative service from Miami. A couple of weeks later Pan Am went bankrupt; their agent in Grand Turk blamed me personally and never spoke to me again. The Cayman Airways service was not without its teething problems. One of its ageing Boeing 727s landed for the first time at the small, ill-equipped but grandly named Grand Turk International Airport and the plane's integral rear steps refused to function. The only available set of steps was wheeled out, but sadly was about four feet too short, so an enterprising member of the airport staff found a workable solution. The tourists, mostly

American, emerged from the plane to find they had to negotiate a small ladder before they reached the actual stairs. I suspect some of them were having doubts about their choice of holiday destination. Nevertheless, TCI went on to have, for the next few years, the highest tourism growth rate in the Caribbean and has developed an excellent, upmarket and profitable tourism industry.

Having set up the Tourist Board I was invited back to be interim Superintendent of Banking and Offshore Finance and Registrar General (in small nations one has to multitask), which was, again, huge fun. On my first day in the office my secretary came in to tell me, 'There's a woman outside want you to marry her'; it took me a while to work out that, as registrar general, I was expected to perform marriage ceremonies. There were also gentlemen in dark glasses and two-tone shoes asking for banking licences and was it okay if they funded it with suitcases full of used banknotes, and much more. My abiding memory of the islands, to which I return every few years, is the laughter; during my time there I laughed a lot. Cried occasionally too.

A few years later I led a team of consultants charged with reviewing the financial services industry in Barbados. On the first day I presented myself to the finance minister to whom we would be reporting. Full of enthusiasm, I bounced in and began to outline our proposed programme and methodology. He let me rabbit on for a few minutes, then lifted his hand and said, in a beautiful, deep, soft Bajan drawl, 'Yeah, man. But take some time to smell de roses.' My type of client. I was newly divorced and Barbados and the Bajans were balm for my soul.

Work in the Caribbean was interspersed with occasional assignments in Eastern Europe, which of course yielded their own memories. My guidebook to Budapest says of the lovely Edwardian Gellert Baths, 'The occasional homosexual advance is easily repulsed,' and sure enough, sitting up to my neck in warm water wearing only the regulation skimpy little apron I felt a hand slide up my thigh and a voice in my ear saying, in

German, that I had nice legs. Dredging up the vocabulary left over from school days I claimed to have a little headache and made my exit. Secretly I was rather chuffed: fifty-five years old and my first gay advance.

I once made a brief visit to Moscow to help prepare a tender for an overhaul of the state health service audit systems. The Oxford group I was representing were partnering with one of the large Russian audit firms and my colleague and I were sitting in their offices to discuss the preparation of our joint proposal.

'How would you like to divide up the work?'

I asked their senior partner.

He replied, in English but with a heavy Russian accent which sadly I can't replicate on these pages:

'We will write the technical submission. We would like you to add the romance, the poetry.'

Only a Russian could see poetry in audit. Being a one-time auditor, should I ever come to write my autobiography 'The Poetry of Audit' must be a contender for a chapter heading.

All of this is irrelevant to this memoir, other than as examples of life causing abrupt changes of plan, as Christina's death was to abruptly change my life. The only relevance is that these were all experiences which shaped me and possibly, just possibly, prepared me for the role I was to play in rebuilding the family business.

At the turn of the century I was still taking on occasional consultancy work, with no expectation that this lifestyle would change. My three daughters were all married, two of them living nearby; my foster-son lived with me, as did my very dependent dog, which my youngest daughter had found a decade earlier in a rescue home in Bahrain. I was, perhaps, a little too comfortable and although I hadn't given the matter much thought I was very ready for another challenge.

At the time Christina died I was fifty-eight years old, living a fairly quiet life in rural Hampshire. My life has sometimes seemed rather more Tom Sharpe than Joanna Trollope but by then I had some of her trimmings, including a four-oven Aga, which the foodie in me misses to this day. My mother, who was a couple of years older than Christina but survived her by a little more than a year, had a modest 8% shareholding in Foyles and after the death of Christina asked that I join the board to represent her, which I did in December 1999. At the first board meeting I attended it was immediately apparent that there was a serious need for additional hands-on management input. I had no knowledge of bookselling but had acquired a range of business skills which could be useful and I had a small flat not far from Charing Cross Road. I had also inherited from both sides of my family perhaps the most useful attribute for taking on the task of rebuilding Foyles, a 'Good Sense Of Humour'.

So, a few days into the twenty-first century I became effectively a full-time executive director of 'the World's Greatest Bookshop'.

6. THE BOOK TRADE

AS A CHARTERED ACCOUNTANT AND one-time investment banker I have had broad business experience, but I had no knowledge of the book trade, a business which defies most commercial logic. On joining the board of Foyles I therefore set out to educate myself. Over a period of several months I invited a few senior publishers to one-on-one lunches. Christina had never engaged with the industry and I suspect that those I asked were so surprised to find a Foyle who wanted to that they accepted. Bit by bit I learnt something about the mysterious but magical process of creating and selling books.

The book trade is unlike any other business I have come across. Its product range is uniquely large and varied. Even before the enormous growth of the self-publishing sector made possible by the internet there were well over 100,000 new titles added to the lists every year in the UK alone and several million technically still in print and available. When I first became involved I was speaking to an old friend who used to own a chain of hardware stores. We were discussing stock control problems and I asked him how many different product lines he had stocked.

'Thirty-five thousand,'

he paused, perhaps expecting me to be impressed.

'We have six hundred thousand,' I commented.

The other side of the volume equation is the tiny number of each title that is printed and sold. The average print run of a hardback is measured in the low thousands, popular paperbacks in tens of thousands. A small bookshop will order one or two copies of most titles, perhaps a couple of dozen of best-sellers. Some years ago I was showing a group of journalists round the Shop and one asked me what the process was if a customer wanted a book which we hadn't got in stock. 'The relevant department will contact the publisher or one of the wholesalers and order a copy. This is added to their next delivery and with luck we have it within a day or two. We then phone the customer who, with more luck, will call in and buy it.'

'And the "profit" on that transaction?' she asked me. Point made, but something I had understood from day one. Just as a scientist will tell you that, technically, a bumblebee should not be able to fly, so a business consultant will tell you that technically bookshops shouldn't be able to trade profitably. But somehow it can and somehow, sometimes, we do.

Although the product range is vast the numbers of people producing this range is comparatively small and at times it seems as if they all know each other. What the book trade lacks in commercial logic it makes up for in its social activities; it is driven by people united by their passion for the product rather than divided by their competitiveness, people who socialize regularly with one another. It took me a while to involve myself socially; I was too busy trying to set up a functional accounting system and a website to do much else. The imperatives of getting the business on a more-or-less even keel overrode everything else and I didn't initially think of myself as in the book trade – I was simply a shareholder with general business experience trying to turn around a failing family business.

Some months after I joined the board I heard a couple of our managers discussing an event they had been invited to that evening, the launch of *The Naked Chef*, the first book by Jamie Oliver. Having a great interest in food and cooking I asked what I needed to do to get on the guest list. 'You're a director of Foyles,' our general manager said, 'of course you will be welcome.' That was the first time I realized what an entrée to the wonderful world of books and publishing my involvement in the business gave me. (At the launch Jamie Oliver, although beginning to enjoy fame through his successful TV series, was sufficiently nervous that he brought his mother along with him and spent much of the evening sitting with her in a corner of the room while the assembled guests, most of them booksellers, enjoyed the publisher's wine.)

After that I began accepting some of the increasing flow of social invitations coming my way. As an industry it is more gender-neutral than any of the other businesses in which I have been involved; although more of the top jobs are still held by men, at the turn of the century three of the four largest publishing houses were run by women. I come from a family of strong women and have always enjoyed the company of women, which to me has a richness and texture not found so often in male company. A dozen years earlier I was an executive director of an investment bank, a male-dominated industry with a very strong macho atmosphere in which I was never completely comfortable; the gender equality of the book trade suited me far better. Some years ago I was telling my oldest daughter about new friends in the book trade and described one of them as an 'alpha male'. To my surprise she hadn't come across the term. I explained. She thought for a while and asked,

'Are you alpha male?'

I said, *'No, of course not.'*

(Hard to be alpha male with three strong-willed sisters.)
She thought for a while longer.

'I know,' she said, *'you're alpha male, with lesbian tendencies.'*

Because of the nature of the industry, dealing as it does with ideas, it tends to attract intelligent people from a range of backgrounds, often in competition but sharing a passion for books. I know of no other industry where there is such an easy social relationship between suppliers, the publishers, and their customers, the booksellers. A surprising number of people working in publishing had started their book-trade careers in Foyles, working for Christina and once I started to join their social world I was, perhaps surprisingly given her reputation as an employer, immediately made welcome.

One of the major social events of the year used to be the Booksellers Association annual conference which, when I first went in 2002, was spread over three days and attended by as many publishers as booksellers. There was serious discussion during the day, serious socializing during the evening and, I suspect, a certain amount of serious fraternizing during the night. It was funded almost entirely by the publishers, who have considerably deeper pockets than booksellers, and culminated in the Book Awards gala dinner. I have been told that, by the time I joined the trade the conference was a shadow of its former self. At my first conference when I came down for breakfast after the gala evening I saw people still at the bar in evening dress, so I can only imagine what earlier conferences must have been like.

In 2002 I was invited to join the board of the Booktrade Charity, then known as the Booktrade Benevolent Society, BTBS. Each year BTBS had a fundraising event known as Walkies, in which teams of publishers and booksellers, usually dressed to represent a book or some other theme, walked from their work places, via ten or so checkpoints, to some central West End bar. Each checkpoint served drinks, usually beer, wine and some made-up cocktail. Foyles, sitting on the edge of Soho, was ideally situated to be a venue, so I volunteered us. A letter I wrote to a terminally ill book-trade friend a couple of years later gives the flavour of the event:

I thought of you on Tuesday when we had the BTBS Walkies. For the 3rd year running we were one of the checkpoints, co-hosting with Colman Getty. As usual it was great fun. Our theme was 'A shared passion for books' which we interpreted as lots of scarlet silk draped around the place, a bright red cocktail of my devising, huge bowls of cherries which I bought in Covent Garden market, and, obscurely, lots of jam doughnuts. We didn't win any prizes, we never will as our budget couldn't match our ambition, but we had great fun.

The evening was, as usual, a varying tide of increasingly inebriated book people. [A lady well known in the trade whose name I won't disclose] arrived with her PA, two dogs and a husband, in that order. She arranged water for the dogs before getting a drink for the husband, but I'm sure that means nothing. Finished at one of the big discos in Leicester Square, where there were three barmen trying manfully to serve 700 thirsty booksellers and publishers. They had run out of white wine by the time we got there – their knowledge of the book trade is obviously limited. Unusually for me I left early and wineless.

* * *

In late 2002 I was invited to speak at the Society of Bookmen (a misnomer which was finally corrected to the Book Society a few years ago). The audience of thirty-two was an all-time low, possibly there wasn't much interest in what a newcomer to the industry had to say about the rejuvenation of his family business, but as a speaker I was given free membership for a year, which I so enjoyed that I have renewed ever since. The membership includes publishers, booksellers, literary agents, authors and others with an involvement in the industry and the Society has ten meetings a year, usually with a good speaker, always with good conversation and often sold out. I know of no other industry-based social club where producers, suppliers, customers and facilitators meet and exchange ideas as openly. Vivienne, my wife, who was chair a few years ago, and I still attend most of them.

The book trade touches peripherally on everything. Most prominent people at some point write at least one book and books are written on every conceivable subject. Through Foyles and other book-trade organizations with which I have become involved I have of course met novelists and poets but I have also met politicians and sports people, heads of state and homeless, lawmakers and criminals – people for whom the only common denominator is that they have written books. Looking back, the book trade has given me great satisfaction and enjoyment in my work, challenges and stimulation, some good friends, many new acquaintances and a wife. No money of course, but that's not the point, is it?

7. TAKING STOCK

CHRISTINA DIED IN JUNE 1999. When the contents of her will became known it was confirmed that she had left her controlling interest in the business and related property company to a charitable trust, as we expected. While she could occasionally be surprisingly generous she was not charitably inclined and did little for charity during her lifetime, but neither was she family minded. I suspect she had a strong but certainly unjustified suspicion of the family and their motives. I suspect also that she saw the business as hers, her baby, her creation and she didn't want or expect it to survive her.

Her executors, two lawyers and her late husband's nephew, sadly to die of cancer the following year, set up the Foyle Foundation with her legacy, a foundation which has since donated tens of millions of pounds to good causes, much of it to promote literacy and the arts.

A few days before she died she had appointed my cousin Christopher, the older son of Richard, to the board and he duly became the third chairman of the business in its ninety-six-year history. Some months later he was joined on the board by his younger brother Anthony. My mother, who had a modest shareholding, asked that I also be made a director, partly to represent her interest in the company but also because she thought with my broad experience I could add value. Thus in late December 1999 I joined the board of a much-loved and once-great family business which few people thought would survive.

In the same month we had the first Annual General Meeting of the company at which all her nieces and nephews, all William Foyle's grandchildren, were present. The meeting was held in Christina's penthouse flat above the Shop, built in the late 1960s. Christina, for all her considerable wealth, was reluctant to spend money and there had been no maintenance carried out for many years. The power sockets were obsolete, Christina having refused to have the 'modern' thirteen-amp sockets installed as this would have required replacing the plugs on all lamps and other appliances. As a result, neither the heating nor the lighting was working. It was a cold December afternoon; we had fan heaters powered from extension leads coming up through the window from the Shop below and for lighting we had a couple of large candelabra on the dining-room table, all adding to the mildly surreal atmosphere.

Apart from an occasional sharp interchange between my sisters, of the sibling type that has continued from childhood, it was a good-natured and enjoyable meeting. We discussed the options. The obvious course of action was to close the Shop, which was running at a considerable loss, and redevelop the site, which was owned by the same shareholders, take our profits and retire. But we all had enormous affection for the business, we were all in our fifties or sixties, had all had interesting lives and enjoyed various degrees of success, and we decided that Grandad's shop deserved another chance. We would do what we could to ensure its survival.

We did not of course inherit Christina's shares; they remained with her executors while they set about creating The Foyle Foundation. Some years later some of the shareholders, myself included, bought them from her estate, at a very full market value: Christina herself would not have made any concessions and her executors reflected that. What we had inherited on her death was not the ownership of the business but the responsibility of its management, a responsibility which she had neglected for a decade or more.

I have a letter, sent in 1995 by a customer, a lecturer at the London School of Economics. The opening paragraphs give a flavour of the business it had become, the management of which we had inherited as the 'noblesse oblige' imposed by a family enterprise:

Dear Sir

Herewith an account of my visit to your 'bookshop' today:
Enter Politics/History Department. Only in Oxfam shops
have I encountered a more tatty, heaped-up, ill-organised set of
merchandise.
I stand helplessly; no one offers service. After unsuccessfully
accosting three people for help (they turn out to be customers), I
appeal to the cashier. She points to the speedily-retreating back
of a ginger-haired youth with a blue T-shirt with 'No. 10' on the
back. There is nothing I can see which distinguishes this youth
as a Foyles employee, save that he looks almost as scruffy as the
department.

It continued in this vein for another page or so.

The building was dilapidated, the staff demoralized and the stock chaotic. Shoplifting was rife, not only the shoplifting that was simple theft but the shoplifting caused by the utter frustration of trying, and failing, to get served. Elizabeth Taylor has confessed to stealing a copy of *A Shropshire Lad* from Foyles, while her husband Richard Burton apparently walked out with a modest collection of Everyman classics; and an MI5 employee was once caught shoplifting books on codebreaking.

At the time of Christina's death I was a freelance consultant, taking on a few assignments a year, all of them overseas. I had some time available and my flat was only ten minutes' walk from Charing Cross Road. I decided to spend a few days in the Shop to see what needed doing and within days I was effectively working there full-time, doing what I could to help rebuild what had been a wonderful family business. I was surprised to be told that, in the six months since Christina died there had been no staff meetings held and that no one had thought to reassure the employees about the future of the company. I was also surprised to find that in the same six months nothing had been done to set up any sort of accounting or management information systems.

On my first full day my younger cousin Anthony showed me round the Shop, at that time home to well over a million books, both new and second-hand. He introduced me to the staff, a diverse mix of long-serving dedicated employees, enthusiastic youngsters and foreign students, who were united by a love of books and, I felt, a deep distrust of the Foyle family. After fifty years of Christina's neglect of their interests and welfare I couldn't blame them. None of them would look me in the eye and I knew I would have to work to gain their trust and also that gaining their trust was essential if the business was to recover.

Some departments looked reasonably smart, indicating a manager with the initiative and subtlety to update without attracting the attention of Christina, to whom change or modernization was anathema. Other departments had obviously been unchanged for decades, monuments to her inflexibility and parsimony. I noticed one particularly grimy window frame on which someone had written with their finger in the thick dust, 'Also available in white'.

Staff working hours coincided exactly with the shop opening hours, nine till six, six days a week; someone had written on the wall by the main door, 'Would the last customer please turn out the lights.' In the first few weeks I spent in the shop I often noticed customers wandering through the departments, books in hand, searching for someone to serve them. I suspect that a number put the books down and gave up and that others pocketed the books and left without paying. It was hard to blame them if they did. Christina had reduced staff numbers as sales fell, her idea of cost control: I charted annual sales against year-end staff numbers for the previous ten years and it was apparent that sales were falling because staff numbers had been reduced and that the business was in a downwards spiral which, if it continued, would inevitably lead to closure. One of my first recommendations was that we should employ more shop-floor staff; we did, and unsurprisingly sales started to pick up.

Being by profession an accountant I started in the accounts department, staffed by a handful of elderly ladies. I asked for the cash book. From memory the dialogue went like this:

'May I see the cash book please?'

'Which one do you want?'

'What cash books do you have?'

'Well, we have seven. The sales cash book, the small accounts cash book, the large accounts cash book, the petty cash book, the foreign cash book, the private ledger cash book and Miss Foyle's private cash book.'

'I want the cash book which shows how much cash we have in the bank account.'

'Ah! You need the bank statements for that.'

I realized that 'the World's Greatest Bookshop', turning over at the time a little under £10m a year, had no proper cash book and didn't know how much cash it had on a day-to-day basis! Fortunately, because of Christina's natural conservatism and reluctance to spend money, and having for many years accumulated profits when Foyles was the dominant British bookshop with little competition, there was still a healthy bank balance. As there was only one small desk-top computer in the whole business I couldn't immediately have a proper accounting system set up; I therefore introduced an eighth cash book and showed the bookkeeping ladies how to use it to summarize the other seven, so at least I could do a bank reconciliation and know how much we had in the bank.

I then spent time in the 'bought ledger' department and watched the lady in charge opening envelopes, taking out suppliers' invoices, screwing them up and putting them in the wastepaper basket. I asked why.

'Well,' she said, 'when the books are received in the basement there's usually a copy of the invoice with them, so we've been told to destroy any invoices coming in by post so the publishers don't get paid twice by mistake.' It was no surprise to find out that publishers frequently put Foyles on stop, refusing to deliver any more books as invoices hadn't been paid.

After a couple of days, on the basis of what I saw in the offices and on the shop floor, I wrote a brief report giving a summary of the business as I found it, very broad suggestions for a recovery strategy and offering to help with the implementation. The offer was accepted and thus, never having expected to work in the family business, I found myself doing so, unpaid and with no formal position. Perhaps not a dream come true as I had never dreamt of doing it, but to my surprise I was helping to run the 'Grandad's shop' of my childhood.

* * *

At the turn of the century, book buyers in London headed for Charing Cross Road, as they had done for a hundred and fifty years and more, and in spite of competition from supermarkets and Amazon it remained the heart of London's bookselling. Foyles was the largest bookshop in the street but there were significant competitors. Next door, on the opposite corner of Manette Street, was a large branch of Waterstones, still occupying the premises Christina had transferred to Tim Waterstone nearly twenty years earlier. Opposite there was the flagship store of Borders UK; a hundred yards away the large and seriously academic London branch of Blackwells of Oxford. Heading south there were many smaller specialist and second-hand bookshops: Zwemmers, Murder One, Silver Moon, Pordes and many more.

To be part of a retail cluster is generally an advantage. Oxford Street with its department stores and shoe shops, Bond Street with its jewellers and Savile Row with its tailors are fine examples of this. Those who suffer within a cluster are the inefficient and by that time Foyles was hopelessly inefficient. Sales were falling at the rate of around 20% a year and customers were turning in exasperation to our far-better-managed competitors. We had a couple of remaining advantages – we had a considerably greater range of stock, for those who cared to search our shelves themselves, and we still had an international reputation, albeit quite faded. There were still some customers, but their loyalty was stretched thin.

It had long been suspected that there was widespread fraud in the shop. When I looked at the most recent audited accounts and compared the gross margins being achieved with the trade discounts given by the publishers, it was blindingly obvious that stock was somehow disappearing without being bought by customers. We started investigating, an investigation carried out mainly by my younger cousin in forensic detail with the help of a major law firm and a professional private investigator.

We discovered that the frauds took many forms, from the manager being persuaded by publishers' representatives to buy unsaleable books, to the open theft of substantial quantities of very saleable books. The former was exemplified by finding, in our first proper stock count, that we had on our shelves twenty-three copies of a Chinese cookery book in Armenian; the latter by new books delivered during the week to our goods yard, being left in their original boxes and then driven out at weekends in unmarked white vans to be taken to a bookseller in Holland.

All this was fairly common knowledge in the book trade but the feeling seemed to be that Foyles was so badly managed by its owners that it deserved what it got. Financial controls were almost non-existent. After her husband's death in 1993 Christina insisted on being the sole bank signatory, but as she didn't want the hassle of actually signing cheques she had made a rubber stamp of her signature which she gave to the manager to use. He was on an annual salary of about £25,000. Enough said.

When fraud was first suspected, in the early 1990s, my younger cousin, who many years before had had some training in accountancy, visited Christina at Beeleigh Abbey and offered his services as an investigator. Apparently he made what Christina considered excessive demands, including a seat on the board, and shortly afterwards he received a phone call from the estate manager at Beeleigh, acting on Christina's instructions. I'm told he said: 'Miss Foyle has asked me to tell you not to write, not to phone, not to visit, just get a job and fuck off!'

The fraud was not restricted to books. As a chartered accountant I looked at purchase invoices with the eye of a one-time auditor. I found, among many other obvious examples of over-invoicing, that we had recently bought 144 boxes of red ballpoint pens, 1,728 in total, 24 for each member of staff! A cursory look in the stationery cupboards revealed many years' supply of post-it notes, paper clips and most other ordinary items of stationery.

Eventually, having gathered enough documentary evidence, our lawyers arranged dawn raids on six or seven of the key perpetrators, including present and past managers, and in a series of court cases we recovered many hundreds of thousands of pounds, a small fraction of the millions which we know had been stolen over a couple of decades, but enough to cover the costs of our lawyers. The company's auditors had been very negligent in not spotting or investigating the indications of fraud which were so blatantly obvious and after the investigation was complete I considered taking legal action against them. I took advice, but decided that, rather than getting bogged down in several years of litigation it would be better, in the long run, to draw a line under the fraud and move on to the more urgent matter of rebuilding the company. The investigation enabled us to suspend the general manager (who, having been found guilty of defrauding his employers, bizarrely took us, unsuccessfully, to the employment tribunal for wrongful dismissal) and to begin the process of employing management staff with the skills needed to help us with this rebuilding.

While the fourth (administration) floor had its population of ladies in their seventies who had managed not to upset Christina, staff turnover on the shop floor had traditionally been high. Christina had had a major brush with trade unions in the mid 1960s when staff went on strike for better pay and conditions. As a result it became her policy to dismiss staff before they acquired any rights or status. Fortunately during the last few years of her life she took so little interest in the business that staff managed to avoid these automatic dismissals and by the time she died there was a nucleus of excellent and dedicated booksellers on which to build, some quietly efficient, some mildly eccentric, a common mix in bookshops.

One of the first specialist departments to have evolved was theology, set up by a Dr Duncan, lay preacher and drinking companion of William's. Since the very early days it was comprehensive and well regarded and for some years it had been run by a youngish man, Jewish by ancestry but catholic by persuasion. It was extremely well stocked. There was an extensive range of loosely theological books on everything from doctrinal Catholicism to Satanism, including the Bible in some twenty-five languages, but the department manager's own prejudices wouldn't allow him to stock a single book on Islam. He was one eccentric who didn't long survive the imposition of proper management.

Because the staff were largely remunerated by commission, sales were still recorded using the procedures introduced by Christina decades earlier, described by some as Kafkaesque, reminiscent of the old GUM stores in Moscow, involving as it did the queueing system so well described by Wendy Cope. The staff commission payments were calculated from the copy invoices retained in their invoice books and Christina had insisted in controlling the entire process. Every week the books were gathered up and her chauffeur drove in from Beeleigh to collect them. Her part-time local staff, working at the Abbey in an unheated and dilapidated outbuilding, then added them up and calculated the commission. After approval by Christina the books and calculation sheets were taken back to London by the chauffeur and delivered to the wages department.

Many months after her death I was looking into the various accounting systems and found that the system had not been changed, the chauffeur still made his weekly run in an old car which I assume was kept for that purpose alone. Because commission was such an important component of staff remuneration the system could not be changed until we had a more rational and fair system in place, which, given all the other priorities, took time and the system therefore continued for many months. It sums up the end of Christina's reign: at the beginning of the twenty-first century, well into the era of electronic communications and computerized payroll calculations, Foyles version of High Speed Data Transport was an elderly Ford Cortina trundling up and down the A12.

Because Christina had had no rapport with staff and had allowed them no initiative, there was complete apathy towards the development of the business, paradoxically alongside a great affection for it because of what it offered to fellow booklovers.

I tried an experiment: I offered the managers of seven of the more successful departments an advertising budget of £10,000 each to promote their departments and asked them to come up with ideas. There was not a single response. It was apparent that as the owners of the business we had to demonstrate our commitment to turning Foyles into an inviting destination before they would cooperate in its regeneration.

The building was in serious need of a major refit but that would have to be done in stages because we could not afford to stop trading for an extended period of time – our reputation with customers was too fragile to risk a temporary disappearance. We asked a couple of architectural practices to produce ideas and quote for a complete makeover. One of them recommended that we turn the central staircase, the structural core of the building, through ninety degrees for aesthetic reasons – they obviously failed to understand the brief and were not chosen. We decided that a retail design firm might have a more practical approach, working closely with our management. They came up with a realistic rolling programme which included rerouting customers up and down the fire stairs for part of the time: it was a mark of the affection in which the shop was still held that we had very few complaints.

During the final years of Christina's reign the stock had spiralled out of control. A mixture of weak management, incompetence, lethargy and fraud had led to chaos. Publishers' representatives had a disproportionate influence on buying decisions and there were areas of the shop where books were displayed by publisher rather than by author or subject. Under the new management we carried out a first winnowing of the stock. Among the titles which went for pulping were two copies of the Building Regulations for 1972, a household medical handbook published in the 1920s which advised pregnant women to avoid 'gusts of passion' and of course the twenty-three copies of the Chinese cookery book in Armenian mentioned above. One of my cousins was sorting through a large dust-covered pile of books in the music department. As the pile slowly shrank a sign was revealed with the words 'Record Department' above an arrow. The fact that we hadn't sold records for several decades was an indication of the age of that particular pile.

For many years one of Foyles' peripheral activities was a lecture agency, in its day very active and representing a number of top speakers including Anthony Hopkins, Tony Benn and Ranulph Fiennes. Sometime in early 1999 a friend, a broadcaster and after-dinner speaker, asked if I had any contacts who could increase his bookings. I of course thought of Foyles and spoke to Kay Whalley, the lady running it, who on the phone was bright, witty and interesting. Nothing came of it; when I became involved in the company I found out why. Kay was approaching eighty, had worked at Foyles for more than fifty years, was rather deaf and almost blind. Her movements, both for their slowness and precision, reminded me of a chameleon, perhaps under light sedation. I asked her what clients the lecture agency had. There was a slight pause, as if for thought: 'We provide speakers for a ladies' luncheon club in Eastbourne. But they haven't met for some years now. It isn't so safe for ladies living on their own to go out any more,' a surprising comment about Eastbourne from a lifelong inhabitant of central London. 'And…?' A further, longer pause: 'That's all, really.'

I then asked the general manager what income the agency generated. He studied his shoes, then looking out of the window said: 'None, really. But Kay helps to open the post.' This of a lady who to all intents and purposes was blind. My initial thoughts were that maybe it was time for her to retire, but after discussions with my cousins we decided that as she had never married and the sole interest of her adult life had been Foyles, 'early' retirement would probably kill her. She therefore remained, a minute, grey-haired little bird of a lady, shuffling round the top-floor offices, a symbol of the continuing eccentricity of the business. Some while later I asked about another elderly lady whose name I found on the payroll. I was told she was Kay's assistant, coming in three days a week to help Kay do the job that had ceased to exist years previously.

Kay lived in a small flat in Shepherd Market in Mayfair, where she'd been a familiar figure for decades. She worked, of her own volition, six days a week and in addition to running the lecture agency had effectively been Christina's personal assistant. Christina would telephone her at any time, day or night, with whatever petty worry she had and Kay would endeavour to sort out whatever needed sorting. Kay discouraged visitors to her own office but took to occasionally coming into mine for a chat, invariably, in spite of my shouted warnings, colliding with a low coffee table I had. She was intelligent and witty, with, on occasion, a very sharp tongue. When she realized that I had no familial affection for Christina she told me how much she disliked her, but her love of Foyles was sufficient compensation for what she had to put up with.

Eventually nature took its course. Kay had been diagnosed with liver cancer but told no one. When one day she didn't come in to work my cousin went round to her flat but in her pride she refused to open the door. She died alone a few days later. We finally had access to her office, which was a glorious mess of paper, unopened envelopes, un-posted letters, every drawer stuffed, every surface covered. It took us weeks to go through it all and many interesting things came to light. We found a postcard which read: 'Dear Miss Foyle, while your bookshop remains a temple to panic, ignorance and suspicion I would prefer not to have lunch with you. Please don't ask me again. Sincerely, Lucian Freud.' We found long-lost share certificates, uncashed cheques, unanswered letters, an unsent cheque made payable to the Inland Revenue for just over £1.3 million, a few mysteries solved. Example after example of waste and incompetence, which would never have been tolerated in a more efficient company, but I know that we were absolutely right not to suggest retirement to Kay. She had died while, in her eyes, still serving the company she had loved since the days of William.

*   *   *

In its heyday Foyles was the pre-eminent English language mail-order bookshop in the UK, probably in the world. It grew to prominence in the 1930s when the British Empire was at its height and there was no television to amuse the many colonial officers spending lonely months in remote parts of the world where bookshops were non-existent. William was always a strong believer in advertising and the messages 'Foyles for Books' and 'Foyles, the World's Greatest Bookshop' were repeated, day after day, in small solus ads on the front page of most of the major British broadsheets.

By the 1950s Foyles was receiving an average of 35,000 letters every day, two mail vans full, from all corners of the world and mail order was a major part of the company's business. The post room had two long tables at which sat a dozen women opening envelopes, extracting cheques, postal orders and banknotes in many different currencies. The money was sent to the cash office, letters to shop-floor staff for action and all postage stamps to the philately department for sale to stamp collectors. As children we would call in on the post room en route to Grandad's office to savour the buzz of gossip; this was my first introduction to the grass roots of business, a visible tide of money flowing in from all over the world, to pay for a tide of books flowing the other way.

Gradually of course competition developed, service fell away and the tide dwindled to a trickle. At its peak, mail order would have accounted, in today's values, for many millions of pounds of sales a year. By the time of Christina's death it was down to an average of a thousand pounds a month and was administered by a single, elderly lady who did all her correspondence in longhand. But she had great pride in what she did and would come into my office regularly to tell me of some small success. I recall one time her saying to me: 'Do you remember I mentioned a customer in New Zealand who'd ordered a gardening book? Well, he was so delighted with it that he's ordered another!' Sale £20, gross profit £7, staff costs probably £50; but customer satisfaction 100%, staff pride enormous. Not a viable business model, but one with its own charm.

The first few months were one revelation of inefficiency after another, adding up to a quite chaotic business which, propped up by the shareholders as landlords, survived because of its fading reputation and, in spite of Christina's appalling employment practices, the excellence and loyalty of the staff. I knew that to attempt to turn it round was an enormous challenge but I did not share the common view that it was impossible. I expected it to be an interesting ride. It was.

Welcome book lover, you are among friends.

8. DEVELOPMENT

HAVING TAKEN STOCK OF THE company we had to stabilize it and begin the process of bringing it into the twenty-first century. The action against fraud resulted in the departure of the general manager and his assistant, clearing the way for us to bring in fresh blood, experienced people prepared to make changes. We recruited a general manager from one of the major bookselling chains, a human resources consultant to help introduce up-to-date employment practices and a financial controller to work with me in installing accounting systems. While this was going on we had to devise a strategy to get where we wanted to be, having first, of course, worked out what we wanted to be.

As part of my education in the business of bookselling I began inviting senior staff for a drink after work, usually in the Pillars of Hercules, a pub on the corner of Manette Street and Greek street where my parents and my grandfather had gone for their after-work drinks, sometimes in the Coach and Horses further down Greek Street, favourite haunt of Jeffery Bernard, Peter Cook and his successors at *Private Eye*. It seemed fitting and I learnt much about the strengths and weaknesses of the staff and, as important, what the staff thought were the strengths and weaknesses of the company. When I told one of my cousins that I had been for a drink after work with some of the staff, I was asked, 'Do you think that was wise?'

At the start of the twenty-first century, bookselling faced many challenges. Books, being readily and uniquely identifiable by their ISBNs, lent themselves perfectly to online selling; e-books were just becoming available; the demise, in the 1990s, of the Net Book Agreement allowed supermarkets and other retailers to sell at cut-price; and the younger generations were growing up in a world that was largely screen-based, giving them access to instant entertainment in many forms.

To survive in this brave and challenging new world we knew we had to reinvent Foyles and evolve into somewhere that, for reasons other than simply wanting to buy books, people wanted to visit. Books are part of the entertainment industry and Foyles had to reflect that. We had to become a destination, somewhere people would come to be entertained, and we had to find a way of monetizing such entertainment – the accountant in me soon found out that profit margins on books are slimmer than in most retail.

We decided that as part of the overall remodelling we would allocate space for a café, but it was not a priority. Our new general manager introduced the idea of staging author events in our gallery, for which people would pay. I remember being pleasantly surprised to learn that people would pay to be given the opportunity to be sold to. Our programme of events grew rapidly, eventually to become as good as any in the country. The list of authors reflected the diversity of our customers and included Maya Angelou and Donna Tartt, Richard Dawkins and Alastair Campbell, Jacqueline Wilson and Terry Pratchett, Robin Cook and Douglas Hurd.

We had to differentiate ourselves from other bookshops and one way of doing this was to play the 'family business' card. In 2001 we decided to have late-night Christmas openings on each Thursday in December and our general manager suggested we serve mince pies and mulled wine. My task was to make the mulled wine, for which I devised an 'old family recipe from

Beeleigh Abbey' and which I and some of the managers, dressed up in dinner jackets and evening dress, served to customers. I made sure those I served knew that I was not just a well-dressed bookseller but also a Foyle. Towards the end of the evening when customer numbers were thinning out I also made sure that all the staff were served, so the evenings had a dual purpose, demonstrating to customers a slight quirkiness and to staff that they also mattered. The following year one of our friendly competitors almost opposite on Charing Cross Road did the same, flattery by imitation.

The obvious way to boost our mail-order business and leverage what remained of our international name recognition was online. A website wasn't high on our priority list but one of my sisters, and a fellow shareholder, is a senior academic with a powerful personality, working in the IT field. She suggested we needed a website; I said we were too busy fire-fighting. She made the suggestion again, more forcibly this time and eventually for the sake of family harmony and conditioned since early childhood to give in to older sisters I agreed to make it a priority. We got several quotes to build a site: they ranged from £1,500 to £600,000. We went for the £1,500 model, from an ex-student of my sister's, highly recommended, and had a working e-commerce website by mid October 2000, not much more than a year after the death of Christina. Given her complete aversion to computers that was, with hindsight, quite an achievement. Foyles had gone from handwritten ledgers to an e-commerce website in less than nine months.

Although the website was set up for automatic fulfilment by one of the major book wholesalers we found that, possibly because of our reputation for service and knowledge, many of the contacts originally made online led to personal follow-up contact by telephone or fax. The mail-order staff (the delightful elderly lady sending gardening books to New Zealand now being 'assisted' by several others) sometimes built up a rapport with individual customers. One such, ex Royal Navy, sent the young lady with whom he had been corresponding a photograph of himself on the deck of his destroyer, taken in 1940 and followed that up with a box of chocolates. That wouldn't have happened at Amazon.

I realized very quickly that being part of Foyles was an entrée to a wonderful industry and that despite Christina's reputation there was great affection in the trade for what was still a very influential central London bookshop. I slowly built up a network of supportive book-trade friends and contacts and through that network came across businesses which would fit with ours and increase our turnover, essential to re-establishing the goodwill of the publishers and improving our trade terms to a level which would enable us to return to profit.

A year after I joined the board I heard, through my growing network, that a mail-order bookselling company, the Good Book Guide, with a substantial mailing list, was for sale. I had a meeting with their business development director and on the basis of that meeting and routine due diligence we made an offer for the business. Unfortunately our offer did not meet the owner's expectations and we were not prepared to pay what we considered an unrealistic price, so we did not pursue the deal. However I had been so impressed with the business development director, Vivienne Wordley, that I made her a separate offer to join us as a consultant and help rebuild our mail-order business, which she accepted. (Many years later having worked with Vivienne at Foyles and in other ventures I made her another offer, that of marriage, which to my great delight she also accepted.)

In early 2001 I went to the awards ceremony for the Orange Prize for Women's Fiction. It was in a marquee on the South Bank on an exceptionally hot evening. A bookselling friend introduced me to two delightful ladies, Sue Butterworth and Jane Cholmeley, the founders and co-owners of the Silver Moon Bookshop, the first feminist and lesbian bookshop in London and probably the best in Europe with a loyal and literary customer base and excellent mail order business. We chatted, got on well and they invited me to join them for dinner, which I did. My family is full of strong women and all my life I have enjoyed the company of women. Jane and Sue were strong, committed, talented and passionate. I remember the dinner being hugely enjoyable with copious quantities of wine and much laughter. We possibly discussed business, and maybe the problems facing book retailers, but as I have only the vaguest of memories of my Tube journey back to my flat around midnight I can't say for sure.

The next day Sue phoned me, explained that for all their jollity the previous evening their business was in a pretty dire situation, unable to pay the rapidly increasing rents demanded by central London landlords. They were unwilling to move to the more affordable suburbs and couldn't continue as an independent bookshop, so would Foyles like to buy them? Given our ownership structure at the time, with a majority of the shares held by the surviving executor of Christina's estate, a very conservative lawyer in his mid eighties, I doubted whether we could persuade the board to buy a very edgy feminist and lesbian bookshop. However, the more I thought about it the more I thought it made sense. Silver Moon had a strong brand, a committed customer base and a mailing list three times the size of ours. Among their customers were many heavy book-buyers, whose reading would range far beyond the feminist and lesbian offering of Silver Moon and who were used to buying their books in Charing Cross Road.

Sue and Jane had already announced that Silver Moon was closing and a party to mark this had been arranged. They wanted a decision quickly, so I put the proposal to the board, describing the business as 'the leading specialist women's bookshop in Europe'. The elderly lawyer, trustee of the Foyle Foundation, asked, 'Apart from books on knitting and cookery, what do they sell?' I gave an anodyne reply and the acquisition was agreed. At Silver Moon's closing party a few days later Sue announced that the business was being acquired by Foyles and a great, spontaneous cheer rang out, a cheer that Silver Moon would continue to exist but also, I think, a cheer that it had found a home in a business which, for all the dreadful lethargy of the last years of Christina's reign, was still highly regarded as a serious bookshop. I joined Sue and Jane and half a dozen others, for a celebratory dinner afterwards. I was the only man.

When, a few months later, Silver Moon reopened on the third floor of Foyles in what had been the Law and Commerce department, it brought with it a slight and welcome edginess and a whole new set of customers who previously would have been unlikely to shop at Foyles. It also sent out a signal that Foyles was once again prepared to explore new avenues, to experiment and to evolve.

*   *   *

This signal was widely heard and had some unexpected consequences. We had decided that as part of our general remodelling we would have a café where the old Maths department had been on the first floor, a café which would say 'Foyles', a café that would be the complete antithesis of the modern chain coffee shops. While we pondered this with no obvious 'concept' presenting itself, I was told that a gentleman from Ray's Jazz had called a couple of times and wanted to talk to me. Ray's, at the top end of Shaftesbury Avenue, was one of the last traditional jazz shops in central London. It had originally been Collet's Jazz, an offshoot of the left-wing bookshop Collet's in Charing Cross Road, but was taken over at some stage by Ray Smith. Ray, facing huge increases in rent and rates, had decided that it was no longer a viable business in its premises in central London, a short walk from Denmark Street, the heart of London's music retailing, and no longer in good health he couldn't face moving to a less appealing location. However one of his staff, Paul Pace, had read that we had saved the Silver Moon Bookshop, another business facing the same problems and thought it worth contacting us.

Out of courtesy I returned the call and explained that we were looking for a café, not a jazz shop. Paul persuaded me to come and talk anyway. Ray's was only a few hundred yards away and I walked over to see him. As I walked in I felt I was stepping back in time: it was dusty, untidy, its furniture care-worn, its few customers, mainly white middle-aged males, looking slightly furtive, and it shouted out 'Old Foyles!' It was quaint and appealing, but it wasn't a café.

Paul, a man of persistence and imagination, wouldn't give up. He showed me a letter of support he had received from the musician Jools Holland in which Jools had said, 'to lose Ray's would be like losing the British Museum, Foyles or the National Gallery'. How could we resist? Paul then took me over the road to the delightful Monmouth Coffee Shop, introduced me to its then manager Jorge Fernandez, keen to start his own venture. Paul suggested that between Foyles, Ray's and Monmouth we could create a terrific jazz café. A great concept, the perfect fit for Foyles with its long tradition of music, problem solved, everybody happy.

But of course nothing is completely straightforward. The designer we were using for the remodelling of the shop was charged with the design of the café and given a brief which he chose to ignore. He was, as usual, late with his designs and when they were finally presented, on a Friday six weeks before the official opening party, they were simply not what we wanted. Smart (and expensive) new hardwood floor, a boringly symmetrical layout of small square tables, the whole concept was devoid of any real atmosphere or personality. A rapid rethink was needed and the designer was not the person to do it. I was going to Cornwall for the weekend with my partner at the time, so we bought some interior design and catering magazines at Paddington and set about brainstorming. She kicked off with 'I have a friend who sells second-hand church furniture' and we went from there.

The following Monday morning Jorge and I went to the quaintly named 'Pew Corner' just outside Guildford and bought seven old church pews and a dozen chairs from redundant churches. Our finance director, who was generally overseeing the renovations, found a craft workshop in the Harrow Road specializing in furniture traditionally made from reclaimed timber to make the tables; and a team of efficient Eastern European workmen renovated the original Victorian pine floorboards. After some tense moments everything came together just in time for the opening party, with a delightfully inebriated George Melly as guest of honour. From day one the combined café and jazz shop looked mellow and totally in keeping with the quirkiness of Foyles and rapidly established itself as a popular meeting place for students, publishers and others. Also within a short space of time a ladies knitting circle had chosen it as their regular meeting place, so perhaps the elderly lawyer had had a point about Silver Moon.

The windows of our new café looked straight into the rather soulless Starbucks in Borders, on the other side of Charing Cross Road, and it was obvious that, in going for the slightly quirky we had created something far more attractive to customers. However, if I looked down to pavement level and watched passing pedestrian traffic being drawn in by the very attractive 'lifestyle' offer of Borders, while they walked straight passed us without a glance it was equally obvious that we still had much to do to draw in customers.

In my search for appropriate acquisitions I discovered that negotiations are sometimes influenced by the most unlikely things. We were invited to bid for the website and bookselling business of the British Medical Association and I went to their premises in Tavistock Square to inspect their records and do the necessary due diligence. I was dressed as I usually am for work, in a fairly casual suit and an open-necked shirt, typical for the book trade and Bloomsbury. The BMA, although in Bloomsbury, obviously had its spiritual home in Harley Street and its staff dressed accordingly. I sensed slight disapproval of my attire spent some hours going through the records without being offered any coffee, the pre-sundown fuel of the book trade. We made an offer, which was rejected. Years later an ex-colleague was talking to one of the BMA senior executives and mentioned that Foyles had once been interested in buying their bookselling business.

'I remember,'

he said. A pause.

'Their director didn't wear a tie.'

On such small things a deal can turn. Recently, over lunch I told that story to Peter Gray, the CEO of John Smith's, one of the major academic booksellers,: Peter told me that John Smith's had been the successful purchaser and that, unusually, he had worn a tie.

We made one more web-based acquisition, with the specific intention of expanding our mail-order business. Very early on we had had conversations with a number of other bookselling businesses to see if there would be possibilities for acquisitions or mergers. One such was Hammicks, a well-respected smallish chain of bookshops mainly in the London suburbs but lacking a central London presence, which we felt might fit well with our one large shop. Nothing came of the discussions but, the book trade being the sociable community it is, I kept in touch with its chief executive. Hammicks was eventually sold and he went on to become chairman of The Bookplace, a business with a strong base of corporate and academic accounts, which eventually came up for sale and which we bought in 2005. This added several hundred thousand pounds of mail-order turnover, much of it institutional, and became the basis of our commercial accounts business, once again a significant and profitable part of the business. Our mail-order sales, which at the time of Christina's death represented a small fraction of 1% of total turnover, are now, enhanced by our web sales, a significant part of the business.

One of the strengths of Foyles in William's day was its combined offer of new and second-hand books, a recognition of the fact that, while titles may go out of print, demand doesn't necessarily stop. Thus, for example, we could offer a fairly complete range of everything written by Winston Churchill, for which there was always great demand. Customers wanting Churchill's works were not unduly worried if some were second-hand. Sadly such a bookshop would seem completely out of place in the twenty-first century. At the time Christina died Foyles was still buying selected second-hand books, sourced by a specialist who we suspected, quite rightly, was adding an unacceptable markup. This was confirmed when he offered us several boxes of a beautiful book on marine life for £20 a copy; he did not know that the book had been written by my then partner specifically for the discount bookshop market where it was widely available for £10. We terminated his services.

We tried to source our own stock, taking a couple of trips to the Book Barn, a huge warehouse near Bristol, in my old Volvo Estate (the same 'pantechnicon' I had used to collect things from Beeleigh Abbey years before), with the heads of a couple of departments which had the highest demand for second-hand. But enjoyable though the trips were to a booklover like me, it was simply not an efficient or cost-effective way of buying. Sometime later I read in the trade press that a well-established second-hand bookseller, Charlie Unsworth, was being driven out of his shop opposite St Pancras Station by ever-rising central London rents. I went to see him and over an excellent fish-and-chip lunch we agreed that he would relocate his business to Foyles. A decade or more later he is still supplying the Charing Cross Road shop.

As a supporter of charities in the very broad area of human rights, my time in Africa had shown me the effect of publicly leading by example and I felt strongly that, if Foyles was seen to have that ethos it would not only benefit charities but enhance our appeal as an ethical organization. William had been philanthropic, supporting, discretely, a number of charities. Christina had left the bulk of her estate for 'charitable purposes' and when I joined the board her 60% shareholding was held by her executors in trust for the Foyle Foundation established under the terms of her will. I suggested that, as part of our corporate social responsibility, we should do our bit for charity and for the next few years, taking suggestions from the staff, we selected two charities each year to support. As the business was trading at a considerable loss this support couldn't be financial, but we did have a lovely gallery space and decided to make it available from time to time for charitable events, without charge.

The first such event, in August 2001, was an exhibition of photographs for Amnesty International, who campaign strongly for freedom of expression, essential to a healthy publishing and bookselling industry. There was a launch party which sticks in my mind, beautiful poetry read by the poet and author Ben Okri to the accompaniment of a gentle saxophone, moving words by actors Anna Carteret and Lynn Farleigh and powerful photographs by Carlos Reyes-Manzo, Jenny Matthews and Howard Davies. It was at that party that I met Soli, a young Palestinian who was to become one of my closest friends. Carlos, who has worked all over the Middle East, introduced us and I was immediately charmed. Soli is of Bedouin background, one of twelve children, and had won a scholarship to a Pestalozzi school in Sussex. When we met he was in his mid twenties, working in the charity sector, intelligent and quietly opinionated, good-looking and naturally charming. Later in the evening I was talking to a middle-aged Jewish lady from North London, also intelligent and opinionated. In the course of our conversation about the apparently insoluble problems of the Middle East I asked if she had ever met a Palestinian:

'Of course not. Where would I?'

'Come with me,'

I said leading her, looking decidedly nervous, across the gallery.

I introduced her to Soli, who turned on his very considerable charm. She almost visibly melted; a little contribution to Middle East peace? Eighteen years later my friendship with Soli is as strong as ever and sadly the Middle East problems are no nearer resolution. There is an old Palestinian joke: Yasser Arafat went to see God and asked him, 'God, will there ever be peace in Palestine?' God looked at him sadly and said, 'Yes, yes, of course, my son, but not during my lifetime.'

During the next few years we had half a dozen photographic exhibitions for Carlos, who became, and remains, a good friend. One, 'The Peoples of Iraq', we deliberately staged just before the invasion of 2003 and somewhat to my surprise the then Development Secretary, Clare Short, who was struggling with her left-wing conscience on whether or not to support the invasion, agreed to open it; another exhibition, 'Under a Shadow – the Children of Iraq', was held a year later, after Carlos had tracked down those of his earlier subjects who had survived; another, for the charity WaterAid, was about drought in Africa; and one was in support of the Saharawi people of Western Sahara, who have lived for more than forty years in refugee camps in south-west Algeria, having been forced out of their homeland by Morocco. They remain there to this day, kept from their ancestral lands by a wall some 1,700 miles long, guarded by the longest continuous minefield in the world with an estimated ten million landmines. The world ignores them.

Homelessness is a major problem in central London

and in 2003 one of our chosen charities was Thamesreach Bondway, now simply Thamesreach, who operate hostels for the homeless. Each evening they send small teams around the streets of London, talking to the homeless and trying to find hostel space for those who want it. I joined them for one such evening outreach patrol and from six till midnight walked from Tottenham Court Road, via the Inns of Court and the Embankment, to Waterloo, talking to a range of homeless people, mainly men, spanning the entire spectrum of class, age and race. It was very much a 'there but for the grace of God' lesson.

Sometime later Thamesreach curated in our gallery an exhibition of art by the homeless. Again there was a party for the opening night, attended by the artists, most of whom were rough sleepers. The quality of the art varied from childish daubs to very competent paintings, but the pride shown by the artists was uniformly huge, each one standing by their own paintings, all of which were reproduced in the modest catalogue we had prepared and all of which sold, at prices ranging from a few pounds to several hundred. I asked one lady, who would not have looked out of place if she had had a sleeping bag over her shoulder, what she would do with the proceeds should her picture, priced at £30, sell. She gave me a dreamy smile and said: 'I'd buy lots, and lots, of chocolate.' I didn't see her again, but as her painting sold I am sure she enjoyed her chocolate.

At charity events we always provided wine and nibbles. For several years we gave the use of the gallery to Poetry London to launch their quarterly magazine. Turnout, for a poetry event, was exceptional, usually well over a hundred. A factor contributing to this was probably the wine which we donated; I learnt that for those poetry events wine consumption was at its highest.

The Literary Luncheons, started seventy years earlier by Christina, were still going strong and I thought it would good to have a Literary Luncheon for children. This we did jointly with the National Literacy Trust, with funding provided by the Foyle

Foundation. It was held at Leith's Restaurant at London Zoo and six local inner London schools each sent a class of 10-11-year-olds, a total of nearly 200 children from all backgrounds, for many of whom books would probably not be readily available and reading wouldn't be a significant part of their everyday life. In addition to the children, there were twenty authors, illustrators and performance poets, scattered around the twenty tables.

Initially most of the children were more impressed with the velvet-covered chairs and the silver service meal than with the authors, but gradually the writers and their words wove their spells. It was an event with a little bit of magic and for months afterwards we saw, in the shop, on the heads of enthusiastic children the red baseball caps which were in the book bag given to each child at the end of the lunch. I still have the letters written by them: 'It was my favourite time ever, the best trip I ever had in the whole live world'; 'It inspired me to write more so I can be a writer when I grow up'; 'Meeting the authors inspired me to read more books and poems' and 'I felt I was a princess.' We sowed some small seeds of inspiration in young minds.

I feel enormously privileged that fate and the accident of birth gave me, at a stage of my life when I could devote time to causes that I care about, the opportunity to stage events in central London on topics that matter. To be able to give a platform to charities which make a difference was hugely satisfying. Having exhibitions of photographs of the effect of the invasion and occupation on the ordinary people of Iraq, without any corporate censorship, was far more effective than donating money. To be able to make a personal statement in public is one of the advantages conferred by a family business.

*   *   *

In 2001 we started a rolling programme of refurbishment which took a couple of years, at the end of which we had a far more functional and greatly improved shop. We installed two new modern lifts to supplement the renovated (but still painfully slow) vehicle of the one-legged Mrs Turner, and our old and illogically placed escalators, the underside of one of which bulged ominously into the basement with decades worth of accumulated lubricating oil, were replaced by rather more elegant open staircases.

As departments were stripped and refurbished some interesting things came to light. Behind the shelving of the Natural History department on the second floor we discovered an old, abandoned lift cage. At some time in the shop's history the lift shaft above and below had been removed, leaving the cage stranded forlornly behind new shelving – Christina had presumably considered it better to waste fifty square feet of potential sales space than to have the expense of dismantling it. Behind the shelving of the Maths department we found a lovely series of cartoons of management, drawn years previously by a perceptive and artistic bookseller. It is strange now to remember that we had an entire department dedicated to Maths and Physics, an indication of the enormous depth of Foyles stock, chaotic though it was.

The jumbled and poorly stocked Children's department was made bright and welcoming. (Christina did not like children very much – in a letter she wrote to me in 1994 she said: 'One thing I shall never be is a grandmother or mother-in-law – thank God!') When it was being refitted we were discussing what we could do to catch the attention of young boys, who generally read less than girls:

'*A fish tank*', said one of my colleagues.

'*Piranhas!*' said Vivienne

and for a dozen years Foyles in Charing Cross Road was the only bookshop in the world with a tank full of piranhas in its Children's department. Feeding time at four o'clock became a regular attraction.

Gradually the book trade began to accept that we were once again a serious bookshop and we were from time to time nominated for awards. The first such nomination was for one of the British Book Awards in 2003, at which we shared the Independent Bookshop of the Year award with the excellent Falmouth Bookseller. It was unusual, possibly unprecedented, for the award to be shared. That we didn't win outright suggests that one or more of the judges simply couldn't accept that we deserved it and that one or more were so supportive that they insisted. Although delighted to have won, knowing how much we still had to do I would probably have been in the first camp. In subsequent years we went on to win many such book industry awards, known in the trade as the Nibbies.

The wider world had also begun to notice that we were coming back to life and the following year we were nominated for the JP Morgan Family Business Honours, held each year at the Old Schoolhouse, a lovely nineteenth-century building on the Embankment at Blackfriars, belonging to the bank. My cousin and I were invited, with our partners, to the awards dinner. My then-partner and I dressed up, me in a dinner jacket, she in a sleeveless long dress. Living in Southampton Row, only a few minutes from the Embankment by taxi, we set off in what should have been good time but it was rush hour and there was not a taxi to be had. Finally, not wanting to arrive late we hailed the only available transport, a bicycle rickshaw, powered by a young Albanian man. I explained that we were in a hurry. '*Ska problém*,' he replied.

I knew from my brief time working in Albania that while *Ska problém* translates literally as 'no problem', it is safer to translate it as 'watch out!' His *problém* was a bent gear wheel and we set off, weaving through the early evening Kingsway traffic, every downward thrust of his right leg jarring the whole vehicle, me shouting directions in his right ear, my partner's carefully arranged long blond hair flying in our slipstream, to arrive at the elegant Old Schoolhouse, the solitary bicycle rickshaw in a long line of limousines and taxis. If not a stylish entrance, it was at least one marked with the slight eccentricity of Foyles. Unsurprisingly, faced with the competition of superbly well-run businesses governed by family councils we won nothing. The dinner was excellent.

The events and exhibitions in our gallery reflected the very broad appeal of books, but in addition we wanted to introduce some modest elements of theatre. This required a fine balance. I have, since childhood, loved Hamleys Regent Street toyshop with young actors entertaining children on the ground floor, but such flamboyance would be too much in a bookshop. Fortunately the configuration of the shop was such that what went on in our front-of-house didn't impact on the rest of the shop. We had, at various times, stilt-walkers in clown costume parading in Charing Cross Road, an actor abseiling down the front of Foyles to launch a new young adult thriller by the prolific writer Anthony Horowitz, a book juggler and the 'Book Grocer' selling second-hand books by weight from a barrow, echoes of William Foyle doing the same three-quarters of a century earlier. Such activities could take place on the ground floor without disturbing the peace of those browsing upstairs.

With all this a new Foyles gradually emerged, a meta-morphosis, from a fusty, run-down and mismanaged old shop into a place people wanted to visit, not just to buy books but to be entertained. By the beginning of 2005 the business had been stabilized and was beginning to be recognized as a destination, once again attracting considerable numbers of book-buyers and potential book-buyers. In March 2005 I tried to sum up what we had become and sent the following email to all staff:

THE WEEK IN FOYLES

In the Gallery on Tuesday we had an event for the cartoons of Robert Crumb which involved, for reasons that will forever remain obscure, his co-author dressed as Zorro, complete with mask and sword, being carried into the room piggy-back by Mrs Crumb.

On Wednesday the quarterly launch event for Poetry London, over a hundred people listening to some excellent (and some not-so-excellent) poetry in a pleasant haze of wine. Some Malaysian gentlemen arrived unannounced and spent over £80,000 on technical books.

On Thursday we had a charity auction for the Free Tibet Campaign during which half a dozen Tibetan monks chanted in full ceremonial robes and which raised over £15,000 for the Campaign, while at the same time there was live jazz in Rays.

I look back on the week and think 'This is the spirit of Foyles, that which makes us not just a good bookshop but a great one' (and some of you read this and think 'What is he going on about?'). But thanks, everyone, and have a nice weekend.

By late 2004 we were ready to expand beyond Charing Cross Road and the management team drew up a set of criteria for possible new branches. They had to be in areas of high footfall, preferably with a tourist component, and they had to feed in to Charing Cross Road while being commercially viable in their own right.

While we were developing these criteria I received a phone call from Jane Cholmeley, one of the original partners of Silver Moon, who had become (and remains) a good friend and who was at the time managing the Borders Bookshop at the Royal Festival Hall:

'Bill, we need to have dinner.'

'When?'

'Tonight.'

We met on the South Bank a few hours later. At dinner in a Greek restaurant overlooking the Thames she told me that the Borders Festival Hall bookshop lease was coming to an end and that they had decided not to renew. It fitted our expansion criteria perfectly and the next morning I sent an expression of interest to the South Bank organization. They responded favourably and we were invited to bid, along with a few other booksellers. Our bid was accepted and in June 2005 the official opening was performed by Sandi Toksvig, broadcaster, stand-up comedienne, book lover and very funny lady. Sandi had been a loyal supporter of Silver Moon and as it was one of the Silver Moon founders who introduced us to the South Bank she was a very appropriate person to officially open Foyles' first new shop in many decades.

The opening wasn't without its comedy. We had decided, for a bit of flamboyance, that we would arrive by speedboat which Sandi, my cousin Christopher and I boarded at Blackfriars. We were flying a Foyles flag from a wooden flagpole at the back of the boat, the river was choppy and we had a fast and bumpy ride upriver. Having fun, we carried on as far as Vauxhall Bridge. When we were directly opposite the MI6 building the flagpole snapped and fell into the water. We immediately throttled right back and circled slowly to recover it. Given the fear of terrorist attacks in London at the time we could almost feel the binoculars focussing on us through the windows of MI6. We retrieved the flag and went back downriver to the South Bank complex where Sandi performed the informal opening ceremony. The shop opened for business the next day, exceeded our expectations and has traded profitably ever since.

Of course, not all of our expansion plans and new developments worked out. Following on the success of the South Bank shop our then chief executive negotiated with Historic Royal Palaces for Foyles to be the booksellers at their various premises, including the Tower of London and Hampton Court Palace. While the locations were a perfect match for our brand we found after some months of operation that they didn't meet the key criterion of making a stand-alone profit. HRP's profit-share requirement was high and the turnover never quite reached our expectations and reluctantly we exercised our right to terminate the agreement.

Also in 2006 we entered into an agreement to take on the bookselling concession at Selfridges in Oxford Street and Manchester. This added significantly to our turnover but traded at a modest loss: Selfridges drove a hard bargain. Attempts to renegotiate were unsuccessful so, again, we terminated the agreement.

In 2006 we decided to tender to become the bookseller at the new Heathrow Terminal 5. The British Airports Association invited interested parties to attend a briefing. I arrived just before it began and took the seat next to an acquaintance of mine, the chief executive of Borders, at that time a thriving chain of 'lifestyle' booksellers. 'What the fuck are you doing here?' he asked in surprise. Neither of us got the contract, but it is worth mentioning that a decade or more later Borders no longer exists while Foyles continues its steady expansion.

Although much of what was done to rebuild this dying business felt at the time fairly haphazard, with the benefit of hindsight I can see a pattern in the various improvements put in place and the reasons for them. It was obvious that the old bookselling model – based on the premise that people only came to a bookshop to buy books, so book range was critical – was not relevant in the multimedia world of the twenty-first century. William, way ahead of his time, had recognized that bookshops needed to do more than just sell books and had added music, stamps, crafts, even a travel agency for those, like me, whose wanderlust was sparked by a book; but Christina had allowed many of those peripheral departments to wither and die. What we had done, over the course of several years, was to change a run-down old building stuffed with books into a place where things happened, which a growing number of supportive customers visited regularly.

It is interesting with hindsight to see how actions have unforeseen consequences, how one thing leads to another. A chance meeting at the Orange Prize awards, as they were then known, led to the acquisition of Silver Moon. The publicity surrounding that eventually led to the acquisition of Ray's Jazz and the setting up of our café. Through the Silver Moon acquisition I became friends with Jane Cholmeley who alerted me to the opportunity at the South Bank. One chance introduction at a social event had contributed directly to the reshaping of the entire business.

Another fortuitous and unexpected chain of events led to the development of our branch at St Pancras Eurostar terminal. Our property company held the lease of a building next door to Foyles, occupied at the time by Central Saint Martins College of Art, with which Foyles had enjoyed friendly relations for many decades. We heard that they were considering moving out and arranged a meeting to explore the possibility of buying their Charing Cross Road building. In the course of the meeting they mentioned that they were planning to relocate the entire University of the Arts, of which Central Saint Martins is a part, to a site being redeveloped at King's Cross. It occurred to me that with some 25,000 students at a single location there might be a market for a branch of Foyles there and I had a meeting with the head of the company developing the site. He told me that the timescale was still not finalized but suggested that the development of the new Eurostar terminal at St Pancras, next door to King's Cross, would be worth considering. He introduced me to the management of the Railtrack retail division and we bid for, and got, premises at St Pancras, opening a branch there in 2008, fittingly on World Book Day.

And two separate chains of events, started when we made our gallery available to Amnesty International for an exhibition, led me, through friendships made at the opening party, to the refugee camps of Western Sahara and to a protest demonstration in East Jerusalem. But those chains meandered beyond the bounds of this memoir and continue still to thread their way through my life.

All these developments helped reverse the decline of the company. In 1999, the last year of Christina's reign, turnover was £9.5m and the operating loss was £846,000. For the year to 30 June 2007 sales had risen to £18m and in a couple of the intervening years the company had actually made modest operating profits, the first such for many years. There was a long way to go, but we were on the right track.

9. PERSONAL MEMORIES

MY INVOLVEMENT WITH FOYLES HAS been stimulating, sometimes stressful, usually fun and occasionally hilarious and has left me with many memories unrelated to the rebuilding of the business but worth recording. Bookshops are wonderful places, some of them models of efficiency, others, like Foyles, with varying degrees of eccentricity. Eccentricity tends to attract eccentrics.

At the end of Christina's reign security on the fourth – administration – floor was non-existent. Most of the visitors were publishers' representatives trying to sell their books to the manager, but anyone could get access. Sometime in June 2000, not long after I joined, I was in the office I had appropriated, struggling to get the bank account reconciled, never an easy task given the chaotic accounting system Christina had left behind, when an elderly man wandered in. Nervous, his eyes darting round the room, sweating profusely, he asked to see the manager.

'He's not here at the moment, can I help?'

A long pause, shifting from foot to foot, his eyes never still,

'Yes. I own this shop. Old Mr Foyle sold it to me twenty years ago.'

'That's strange. He was my grandfather and never mentioned any sale to me.'

Another long pause.

'Old Mr Foyle sold it to me. I had a flat in Trafalgar Square. He took that. There were diamonds in it. I paid him £800,000.'

Some more of this and I gently ushered him out, never to see him again.

Around the same time, while in my office, I heard an aggressive customer berating one of the staff over some problem. I found out later he had tripped over the slightly irregular but clearly marked bottom step of the central staircase. Eventually the manager intervened and after trying calm reasoning, which was met by increasing complaint, said,

'Perhaps you should consult a solicitor.'

'I am a fucking solicitor!' came the reply.

We didn't hear any more.

The staff, by and large, are a compassionate group and I recall a slightly surreal episode in the shop. One miserable day in late 2000 a pigeon with a damaged wing was found in the goods yard. This was duly reported to the fourth floor and Esther, the elderly Philippina bookkeeper who I had earlier found binning all the suppliers' invoices, decided it needed food. She went to a local coffee shop to buy it a croissant, assuming Soho pigeons to be quite sophisticated:

'Do you want butter with that?' she was asked.

'Of course not, it's for a bird,'

she replied in her fairly abrupt manner, leaving the waitress thoroughly confused. Attempts to feed the bird proved unsuccessful. An SOS was sent out and eventually a lady arrived from a pigeon rescue home in Wimbledon (where else?) with a wicker basket. But too late, the bird was dead. She said to our then general manager,

'But thank you for caring. Where is the body?'

to which the general manager replied,

'In the wheelie bin, of course!'

One very disillusioned lady returned to Wimbledon.

The range of knowledge contained within the shop is not limited to the books. The staff are highly educated and have their own specialist expertise. The gentleman running the very successful 'English as a foreign language' department, still with the company after more than fifty years' service, is as knowledgeable as anyone on books on English grammar, one of which was for decades Foyles single best-selling title after the Bible. A customer on the ground floor asked one of the booksellers if he knew who had written *The Frogs*. The young man didn't know but immediately called his colleague in EFL, known throughout the shop for his classical knowledge, in his second-floor department. 'Euripides,' he said, and as he hung up he realized his mistake. Jumping up from behind his desk he took the central stairs two at a time, calling out in his stentorian voice, 'It was Aristophanes, it was Aristophanes!' to the puzzlement of customers.

In another less dramatic but equally impressive demonstration of the specialist knowledge of the staff, I had read a review of a new biography of Ibn Battuta, a Moroccan explorer of the fourteenth century not widely known in the UK but in whom I had an interest as my brother-in-law's boat was named after him. I asked the lady running the Archaelogy department if we had it in stock. 'Yes,' she replied, 'but there was an American biography of him written about ten years ago which I think you'll find is rather better.' It is this level of knowledge which had kept customers coming back to Foyles in spite of the otherwise appalling service. Incidentally my brother-in-law, who lived in Kuwait at the time, had originally wanted to name the boat *Bukra, insh'Allah* ('Tomorrow, God willing'), the loose Arabic equivalent to *Mañana*, because of the interminable delays in dealing with the civil service over its import. The authorities refused to allow the name.

During the years after Christina's death news spread that we were rejuvenating the company and that the new management obviously cared about the company's reputation. We had many letters from customers, some congratulating us, several from people whose guilty consciences were obviously pricked, ex-shoplifters moved to send us cheques to make amends, including one from a gentleman in India enclosing $100. One letter reminded us of how things had been: 'A few years ago I went to Foyles and bought a book. I was so exasperated by the amount of walking up and down stairs that I had to do, that I turned to the charming German sales girl and said, "This is the worst bookshop in the world." She replied, "I agree with you."'

William had wanted to build a bookshop with universal appeal and although Foyles has never had, or wanted to have, the 'class' of Hatchards with its royal warrant, it has had many royal visitors. In the 1930s 'Old Queen Mary', as the wife of King George V became known, visited. Like many of the Royal Family she never carried money and when she decided to visit central London shops word spread and high-value items were hidden away.

Although there is no record of other members of the British Royal Family visiting, in 2002 the Foyle Foundation made a substantial grant to the King's College Library in Chancery Lane. It was opened by the Queen and my sisters, cousins and I were presented to her. The opening coincided with a strike by the postgraduates at King's College London which my sister Margaret, a professor at King's College, supported. She was on the picket line sporting a very large picket's badge. The Queen and Prince Philip arrived in their Rolls-Royce and were loudly heckled by the pickets. Margaret left the line and sprinted (as much as a lady of her traditional build can sprint) inside for the presentation. Prince Philip spotted the badge and light banter ensued. I was, unusually, tongue-tied.

In late 2002 King Abdullah of Jordan and King Gyanendra of Nepal were both seen, on successive weekends, in our Military History department, generally considered one of the best stocked in the world and at the time in our top three departments for sales per square foot. King Gyanendra had acceded to the throne a year or so earlier following the massacre of many of his family; Abdullah had fairly recently become king after his father Hussein died. When heads of state from unstable parts of the world shop in our military department we know that all is not necessarily rosy in their countries. It is possible to make educated guesses about potential world events from people seen in the Shop. In January 2003 the US Embassy bought our entire stock of road maps of Iraq and the UK Ministry of Defence bought several books on the laws of war; we suspected, correctly, that the invasion of Iraq was imminent.

One Saturday afternoon some years later the gentleman running our English Language department was engrossed in his idiosyncratic and outdated but still efficient index card stock-control system. He has a powerful voice and a tendency to appear rather abrupt, which doesn't at all reflect his true character. Looking up, he saw a middle-aged couple standing in front of him, waiting patiently to get his attention. 'Aren't you the King of Spain?' he barked. 'Yes', said the customer, nodding nervously, used to rather more deferential treatment.

One of our staff members, Faiza, a very well-connected young lady of Pakistani origin, was invited to attend a royal wedding in Jordan. Apparently even at such a prestigious event there are buffets and buffets generate queues. In one such queue Faiza found herself standing next to a beautiful and elegant lady, who asked her where she was from and what she did.

'London. I work in a bookshop.'

'Waterstones?' asked the elegant lady.

'No, Foyles.'

'Ah, so much better.'

'And what do you do?' asked Faiza.

'I'm the Queen of Morocco.'

Nice to know that we are so well regarded by royalty, even if not patronized by our own. We had other visitors, in their own way almost royalty. One wet Tuesday afternoon in 2002 we had a phone call:

'This is Nelson Mandela's PA. He is in London on a private visit and would like to come to Foyles.'

I arranged for his car to have access to our goods yard and for our assistant manager to greet him. We had been told that his main interests were Politics, History and Current Affairs, so he was taken up to the second floor in the wonderful old wood-lined goods lift carved with the graffiti of the previous seventy years. I met him, introduced myself and left him to browse, which he did for a couple of hours, buying a number of books including a selection of crime fiction. It is interesting that, tall and distinctive as he was, no one troubled him or attempted to speak to him. For me that was the high point of all my interactions with customers.

On another Saturday afternoon when the shop was quiet Michael Jackson came in and selected a number of books, mostly on film production, with a combined value of something over £1,200. He asked the star-struck bookseller to deliver them to his hotel, saying that the hotel would pay on delivery, which of course they didn't. It took us more than two years to get payment and then only on threat of legal action.

In 2004 Bill Clinton came to the UK for a publicity tour to launch his book and I was among the few hundred book-trade people invited to his publisher's party. As we were getting ready to leave and departing guests were saying their goodbyes to the ex-President I was with a group of friends including Jacqueline Wilson, one of our most successful children's authors. I made some comment about Clinton needing to meet the greatest living children's writer and thrust Jacky upon him. They spoke briefly, then I, with champagne-induced courage, thought 'my turn', introduced myself and shook his hand. 'Ah, Foyles,' he said, 'mah favourite bookstore!' I was later sent a picture of our meeting and, consummate politician that he is, his expression suggests that he had been looking forward to our meeting for years.

*　　*　　*

The Literary Luncheons continued for some years after Christina's death and in late 2003 we had one for two powerful women, Kate Adie, the redoubtable BBC war correspondent and Madeleine Albright, who had been Secretary of State under President Clinton. A fierce, slightly reptilian-looking lady, she had made a cruel and unforgettable remark, which she later deeply regretted, about the deaths of children in Iraq caused by sanctions which prevented medicine from being available, as being 'a price worth paying'. She arrived at the Dorchester where the lunch was held, with her two security guards with ill-concealed guns under their suits, and looked quite lost. I went up and introduced myself and as she still looked lost I instinctively put my arm round her shoulders and gave a little squeeze. She relaxed and softened into me and I realized that, under the necessarily tough exterior she was a warm and vulnerable person. Probably the only time I will cuddle a Secretary of State.

Although unable to play an instrument or to sing in tune I have a great love of music and I have some moving musical memories of Foyles, which for the past hundred years has had a strong music offering, in books, recorded music, musical instruments and latterly Ray's Jazz.

At the seventieth anniversary Literary Luncheon held in October 2000 there were some 500 guests, predominantly middle-class English people. One of the speakers was the late Larry Adler, then aged eighty-seven, who made his name, mainly with the same demographic, playing the harmonica in the 1930s and 1940s. When his turn came to speak he stood up, produced a harmonica and began to play 'If You Were the Only Girl in the World', which so resonated with the audience that almost all joined in. The sound of 500 elderly people, all lost in their own memories, singing softly in unison, added an unexpected little bit of magic to a memorable occasion. It was Larry Adler's last public appearance – he died a few months later.

In 2004 we had a book launch in our gallery for a biography of Billie Holiday, Lady Day. After readings by the author the audience all went one floor down to Ray's Jazz café where a singer sang some of Lady Day's repertoire, the wonderful music of the 1930s. A moving musical evening which few bookshops could have staged.

The background music to my teenage tears was Trad, British traditional jazz, Chris Barber, Monty Sunshine and of course Humphrey Lyttleton and I was delighted to find, when going through our archive photos, an old black-and-white print of the Humphrey Lyttleton band playing on the roof of Foyles. We worked out that it had been taken in 1951. A little more than fifty years later one member of that band, the clarinetist

Wally Fawkes, also known as Trog, the *Daily Mail* cartoonist, was one of the many top musicians who played in Ray's Jazz.

There are many small moments of magic in any bookshop, moments of discovery, making that unexpected connection with an author either vicariously or directly at a book signing or reading, increasingly part of bookshop life. We had an event in the Foyles gallery for Garrison Keillor. Sitting in the front row was a mother with her son, perhaps ten years old. When it came to questions the boy asked Garrison about his poem about a cat. Garrison looked directly at the boy and, in his best 'Lake Wobegon' voice, said: 'Do you mean "My cat she pleaded and my cat she cried . . ."' and continued, making unbroken eye contact with the young boy, to recite all eighty-six lines. The boy sat spellbound and for a few minutes the rest of us didn't exist for either of them. A child was inspired.

Incidentally, while checking on the poem I came across another Garrison Keillor poem about a cat, which begins:

We miss her gentleness and grace,
The little eyes, the solemn face.
The tail flicking where she lay
on a square of sun on a summer day.

Having lost a cat a couple of years ago, that revived memories. Our world is so enriched by reading and by words which, when arranged so beautifully, bring memories, if not cats, back to life. Half the population never read books: they miss so much.

A smaller moment of magic for me, at one of our events. Some years before his death we were hosting the wonderful Terry Pratchett. In the Green Room beforehand our events manager introduced me: 'This is Bill Samuel, a director of Foyles.' Terry fell to his knees, clasped his hands together and said: 'A director of Foyles!' I fell to my knees facing him, clasped my hands together and said, 'Terry Pratchett!' Authors can be superstars and they provide the books which draw the customers into our shop, but it was nice to have the recognition from one of the best, that we booksellers are, in our modest way, also important to them.

My involvement with Foyles enriched my life in many ways, some unconnected with the business. After years, decades, of Foyles being mocked by the media as an outmoded and mismanaged business we were, a couple of years after Christina's death, beginning to attract kinder press coverage. One visit by the press had, for me, very unexpected and delightful consequences. In September 2004 I showed a party of foreign Journalists around the Shop and remarked to a Finnish lady that 'when I was eighteen I was in love with a Finnish girl, but eventually we lost contact.' About a month later I received a letter from Finland and knew immediately that it was from my 'Finnish girl', Marikka.

She gave her contact details and I immediately telephoned her. A few weeks later she came to London, ostensibly to visit her aunt, but mainly, I think, to see me. Our meeting, in the foyer of her hotel, was extraordinarily emotional. We had last seen each other forty-five years earlier, when she was sixteen, I was eighteen. We stood and held hands and locked eyes and those years rolled away in the loudest and most intense of silences, broken only when Marikka said, 'If I don't sit down I'll fall down.' I had rediscovered a long-lost friend and felt like I had gained a sister. She told me that a few weeks earlier she had returned from holiday to find a large pile of accumulated newspapers in her post box. She was going to throw them all away but on impulse decided to keep the Arts section of the latest Sunday paper, opened it up and saw, on the front page, a picture of me in Foyles, with an article about the rejuvenated shop. She said to herself, 'That's my Bill' and wrote the letter.

Some years later in a bitterly cold February I visited her in Finland. She collected me from the airport and drove me through the snow to her home in Kouvola, in the East near the Russian border, and we caught up on the fifty years that had elapsed since we first met at Saunton Sands Hotel in North Devon. We pottered amiably around her house, prepared food together and the years melted away. I had rediscovered a child-hood friend and the teenage love we had enjoyed half a century before was reborn as a wonderful platonic, adult friendship. We remain the best of friends, corresponding regularly.

*   *   *

With a couple of years of profitable trading under our belt, we were considering opportunities to leverage the brand. One idea discussed was the possibility of franchising overseas. Having spent many years visiting and eventually living in the Arabian Gulf I had friends in Dubai, whom I used to visit from time to time when en route to holidays further east. On one such visit I made a point of touring the bookshops to get a feel for the market and possible franchise partners. I met and became friends with Dubai's most successful bookseller, Isobel Abulhoul, an English lady who had married and settled in Dubai some forty years earlier, whose business, Magrudy's, had a dozen or so bookshops in the UAE.

On a subsequent visit, in early 2007, I was having coffee with Isobel, discussing among other things all the festivals held in Dubai: a film festival, an art festival, a food festival, even a shopping festival (it was Dubai, after all). A friend who was with us said, 'But there isn't a literary festival.' Isobel and I looked at each other, obviously with an identical thought: why not set up the Foyles/Magrudy's Literary Festival? My imagination, coloured by thirty years of working in and around the Gulf, envisaged a Bedouin tent among some undulating dunes, thick carpets, aromatic coffee and a small number of charismatic authors. Little did I know!

I returned to London and filed it away into the Great Ideas Unlikely to Happen pending tray in my mind. A week or so later Isobel had coffee with one of her good friends, Audrey

Flannagan, whose husband Maurice was the chief executive of, and driving force behind, Emirates Airline. I understand that their conversation went something like this:

Audrey: *'Magrudy's ought to have literary luncheons like those Christina Foyle had in London.'*

Isobel: *'Interesting you should say that: I had coffee last week with Christina's nephew and he suggested we have a literary festival in Dubai.'*

Audrey: *'What a good idea. Talk to Maurice, he may fund it.'*

She did so and a few days later called me and said,

'Bill, do you remember the idea of a literary festival?
Well, Emirates are giving us funding!'

My immediate thought was

'Oh shit, what do we do now?'

But then I thought

'Why not?'

And so the Emirates Airline Festival of Literature, which was to grow into one of the most successful of the many international literary festivals, was born, as an illegitimate child of Christina's literary luncheons – one thing leading, by a circuitous route, to another. Someday the full story of the Festival may be told but this is not the place for it. However, of my many memories I'll note a few, to give the flavour of this indirect offspring of the Foyles Luncheons.

It almost didn't happen. Shortly before the first Festival an author, whose book we had tactfully rejected as it simply wasn't very good, seeing an opportunity to get publicity, accused us of censorship. One of the best-known authors who had agreed to appear was Margaret Atwood, at that time the President of International PEN, the authors' charity which campaigns among other things for freedom of speech. She read of this in the *Toronto Globe and Mail* and immediately and vocally and publicly pulled out of the festival. Others threatened to follow suit. We had many international calls between Dubai, London and Toronto where Atwood lives and eventually we brought the Festival back on track. She subsequently wrote a fulsome apology, published in *The Guardian*, in which she says that she had been 'stampeded into a misconception' by a publicity campaign for the book, 'jumped on her white charger' and was left with 'egg all over her face'. We added to the festival programme a debate on censorship, with a panel including several authors who had been subject to censorship in their home countries and a senior UAE government minister, with Margaret Atwood taking part by video link. She appeared in person the following year.

Apart from trying to persuade UK-based authors that a literary festival in Dubai was not an oxymoron, my role in the Festival was largely undefined: I tried to make sure that nothing went wrong, which among other things involved organizing the authors' flights and travel arrangements. Most of them were a delight to deal with: one, a prolific novelist with an aristocratic background, described me as 'a most distinguished ticketing clerk'. Some were less easy. The most difficult was an American economist of Lebanese descent who had written one very successful book predicting the financial meltdown of 2008. As with almost all of our authors he was to travel business class (Emirates Airline gave us two business class tickets for each of our authors). On receipt of his ticket he immediately called me from Washington, on my mobile, late one evening our time:

'Beel, I have received my tickets. You have booked me business class. Beel, I am very important man, adviser to the President, I only travel first class. If you want important men like me at your festival you will change to first class, thank you, goodbye.'

Needless to say I did not change his ticket and he duly arrived, full of his own importance. A few days later I found myself standing next to him in the toilets, a changed man:

'Beel, this has been the most amazing time, I have met some wonderful authors, heard some amazing talks, thank you, Beel, so much!'

It's always nice to see academics gently dislodged from their perches.

I spent much of the time going round the staff and volunteers, reassuring them and encouraging them in any way I could. Being a physical person I do this partly by the occasional touch, a hand on the shoulder, a hug. At the end of the second Festival one of them, Mia, short and stout, hard-working and efficient, put an arm round my waist and her head on my chest, leant into me and said, in the sweetest, gentlest voice, *'Mister Bill, Mister Bill'*, sighed and went back to work.

From year one the Festival has had a significant educational programme, sending all the authors out into schools to talk to students. It has influenced thousands of children and encouraged them to read. It has had other educational benefits, educating Western writers into the ways of the Gulf, replacing the common misconceptions spread by some of the media with the reality of a rich and ancient culture. It now has official backing from the Dubai government and goes from strength to strength.

As I mine my press cuttings for memories one comes

up, something from my varied past life, nothing to do with the book trade apart from giving rise to a photograph which somehow was picked up by the trade press. In 1995 the chief minister of the Turks and Caicos Islands had asked me to be their government representative in London. Some of the UK Overseas Territories had fully staffed London offices: the smaller ones had an individual to represent them. Between us we set up the UK Overseas Territories Association, to offer a united front in dealing with the Foreign Office and DfID, both highly skilled in the art of divide and rule. In 2002 TCI took part in the Commonwealth Games, which that year was held in Manchester, for the first time. Their team was managed by an old friend and one-time beach-front neighbour Rita, by now a senior civil servant in the department charged with managing their very small contingent of four competitors. Rita asked me to join them in the opening ceremony to swell the numbers.

I arrived at the Games Village Hotel, met up with Rita and her colleague Julia and was given my 'TCI national dress'. The population of the islands is mainly descended from slaves and, having been at various times a dependency of Bermuda, the Bahamas, Jamaica and the UK, 'national identity' is not clear-cut. A couple of years earlier the TCI government had felt the need to reinforce national identity by creating a national dress and commissioned the Head of Culture, David, a gay ballet dancer recently returned from Japan, to design one. The result was a loose-fitting white satin suit with multicoloured hoops on the arms and very large buttons down the front. I took mine up to my room and tried it on with great and justified trepidation. I not only looked like a pregnant clown but the trousers were several inches too long and I had visions of tripping up as I marched past the Queen.

I took a bus into town to buy needle and thread and although needlework is very far from my strongest suit I managed to shorten the trouser legs. I put on the costume, looked at myself in the mirror, had a laugh and a couple of stiff gin and tonics and went down to meet the rest of the team. Feeling like an idiot the only consoling thought I had was that, in the Athletes Village of the Commonwealth Games, I was very unlikely to meet anyone who knew me. In the lobby I met Rita and Julia, two lovely, short, dark-skinned ladies wearing the female equivalent, white dresses with flouncy skirts with multicoloured hoops. They looked stunning. I stood between them, towering over them, a pale white thorn between two beautiful black roses and we set off for the stadium, where we were the most photographed team in the games, our picture appearing on the front page of the village daily paper *The Games News* the following day, next to that of the Queen.

The ceremony itself was surreal, marching round a stadium in a satin clown suit, in front of 60,000 people, cameras flashing everywhere, making occasional eye contact with someone sitting way back: it is impossible to explain but there were times when I locked eyes with a single individual and everyone else disappeared for a few seconds, then the moment was gone. The ceremony finished with all the thousands of competitors dancing in the middle of the stadium, a happy multinational multiracial crowd, relaxed and joyful. It was a very special occasion the likes of which I, as a non-athlete, had never expected to experience.

I've heard many authors, talking of their writing experience, saying that the characters take over the plot and implying that the direction of the prose is outside their control. I fear that my memories are doing the same, so I'll return to the main narrative.

10. ALL GOOD THINGS

IN MAY 2004 I TREKKED with my youngest daughter and her husband to Annapurna Base Camp in the Himalayas. After eight fairly exhausting days we arrived back at the main road where we were to be collected, at noon on a cloudless day when the temperature had soared to more than thirty degrees, having been minus five three thousand metres higher up the mountain three days earlier. My exhausted body had gradually relaxed as we strolled down the last stretch of mountain track, knowing that there would be a minibus waiting to take us back to Pokhara, where in turn there would be several cold beers waiting.

The road was ominously quiet, not a minibus in sight. Our guide Jagan was told that Maoist guerrillas were active in the area and had blocked all traffic. It was forty-five kilometres back to Pokhara and I asked him what we should do. 'We walk.' I asked how long. 'Two and a half days.' In fact it turned out to be only one and a half, but the start of the walk involved an ascent of 500 metres in the stifling heat, using up the last of my physical reserves. Fortunately, once we had crested the ridge it was a beautiful, long, slow and gentle descent, through lush woodland, nothing to do but put one foot in front of the other for several hours.

It was a wonderful walk, during which I meditated and

used the time to think about the direction of my life. That evening in the primitive guest house, confined to my room by my daughter who didn't trust me not to get into conversation with the Maoists, I wrote in my journal a short list of 'life-decisions', the first of which was: *Leave the development of Foyles to others. I can inspire but not implement. (Elaboration: I've done as much as I can, as an amateur, in hands-on stuff. Time for the professionals to take over. The next stage will be done over a timescale of ten years or so, too long for a 63-year-old; all I can do is feed my vision to others.)*

Of course, as with the other resolutions, including the one which said, 'drink more water and less wine', it proved at the time to be impossible. But I was beginning to recognize that the days of my active involvement were limited. I should mention that when we finally reached Pokhara after a three-hour row across the lake in a very leaky boat, we stayed in the lovely Fish Tail Lodge right beside the lake. The following night it was blown up by the Maoists, so my daughter was probably sensible to prevent me from meeting them.

At the beginning of that year we had appointed a chief executive with considerable experience of retail, mainly in the music and entertainment industry, which faced very similar challenges to bookselling. A year or so later he was joined on the board by Vivienne and the finance director who had been with the company since a few months after I joined. The board then had the skills needed for all the day-to-day running of the company and my role was limited to strategy and longer-term planning which I enjoyed – I have never claimed to have any retailing skills. With a balanced board there was a period of growth and steady development. We opened our branches at the Royal Festival Hall, the St Pancras Eurostar Terminal, Selfridges and the Historic Royal Palaces and we strengthened our web and mail-order business with the acquisition of The Bookplace. The company had produced operating profits in the years to June 2004 and 2005, the first such in many years, and although the London bombings of July 2005 severely impacted business I felt that we had at last a sustainable business, a strategy for its development and a competent management team which could be expanded as the business grew.

The other shareholders did not have the same confidence and eventually the decision to back off was taken for me and my influence over the development of what I had always thought of as a family business was brought to an abrupt end. In April 2007 my cousin Christopher Foyle, as majority shareholder, informed me that he was bringing in a new chief executive and I was very definitely to take a back seat. A year later he relocated to Monaco and requested that I relinquish my title of vice chairman. We discussed the appointment of non-executive directors and while I argued for someone with retail experience he appointed an accountant friend with whom he had worked for many years. By then we had four accountants on the board, including the new chief executive, and it was to be another six years before my suggestion that the board be strengthened by the addition of a retailer was implemented.

It soon became apparent that the new chief executive and I had different visions for the future of the company. I disagreed with his new strategy of expanding by opening branches in shopping malls and outside London: some years earlier we had agreed to concentrate on Charing Cross Road and central London satellites in areas of high footfall and tourist interest. I also disagreed with his decision to shelve any further development of our website and online sales in favour of traditional bricks-and-mortar retail. So I stepped aside and watched the strategy change, mutate rather than evolve, and from then on my influence was limited to participation in monthly board meetings where, largely because my vision for the company differed significantly from that of the other board members, I was frequently in a minority of one.

There were subtle changes too in the character of the business. One such, significant for me, was the discontinuing of our support for charities, the reason given being that not many books were sold at charitable events. I argued that by hosting free charitable events we were sending out signals about the ethos of Foyles, which would appeal to and expand our customer base, and that people attending such events tended to be book-buyers. I was overruled. Fortunately, however, the Foyle Foundation, established under the terms of Christina's will from the fortune built up by William, continues to donate several million pounds each year to good causes, many of them related to literacy.

The book trade had by then recognized that Foyles was once more a significant presence in the industry. I was invited by a publisher to the 2008 Book Awards – Foyles had taken a table but I had not been invited to join it. A couple of days before the ceremony the managing director of *Publishing News*, the sponsors of the awards, called me and asked if I was going as, she said, they wanted a 'real Foyle' to be there. I guessed that meant Foyles would get an award, which turned out to be that for Independent Bookseller of the Year.

The entire Foyles table went up to the podium and I followed. After the formal routine acceptance by the chief executive I made an impromptu speech, more personal and more heartfelt, about the joys of rebuilding 'Grandad's shop', during which my voice cracked a couple of times and I suspect the audience understood why. We went on to win the Bookselling Company of the Year, chosen from the winners of three separate categories and I gave part two of my impromptu speech. It was my final exit from any active involvement in the day-to-day of the business, but I took great satisfaction in the part I had played in turning a chaotic, inefficient and dying family business into a more diverse and rounded retailer with the momentum to carry it forward through the twenty-first century, and in that part being publicly recognized.

I continued to sit on the board of the company as a non-executive director, aware that there was still much to do. One by one the competing Charing Cross Road bookshops had disappeared. Waterstones, for a couple of decades our neighbour across the road in Manette Street, had relocated their branch to Oxford Street, Borders opposite had gone into liquidation, Blackwells eventually closed their branch just down the road. Of the large Charing Cross Road bookshops, Foyles, thought by most at the turn of the century to be a dying business, was the last man standing. While there were some benefits to the disappearance of competition there was also a significant downside: Charing Cross Road was no longer the heart of central London bookselling. And improved though the business was, its flagship store was still housed in an inefficient collection of old buildings where the only improvements that could be made were purely cosmetic. On its own it was not enough to bring book-buyers to the street. It had become obvious that the shop had to be rehoused in a building which would of itself be a big enough attraction to draw visitors.

When we inherited our shares in Foyles we also inherited shares in Noved Investment Company, the company which owned the flagship store plus some adjacent properties, including a long leasehold of part of the premises occupied by Central Saint Martins College of Art. Through this connection we had heard, towards the end of 2002, that the University of the Arts, the parent body of Central Saint Martins, was planning to bring together its various campuses at a single site at King's Cross. In October 2002 my cousins and I met the University property team to express our interest in taking over their Charing Cross Road premises when they moved out. We were shown round and asked architects to assess the building's suitability as a future home for Foyles. Some outline sketches were produced, showing how the building, in serious need of complete renovation, could look if gutted, rebuilt and opened up.

It seemed ideal and from then on our property strategy focussed on the rehousing of the flagship store in the Central Saint Martins building. The dialogue with the university continued for several years while their plans were inevitably delayed and central London property market values fluctuated wildly, but eventually, in 2010, we acquired the iconic 1930s building which was to become Foyles' new home. We had a parallel dialogue with the Westminster department of planning to allow the change of use from educational to retail, helped by the fact that a significant proportion of our business was in educational books and we were still the bookshop of choice for many of London's university students; the change of use was granted a year or so after we bought the building.

The management, supported by the other non-executive director, initially disagreed with the proposed move, arguing that the flagship should be relocated in a purpose-built retail building with on-site delivery and storage provision, at a more affordable rent, which would have required the flagship to be outside the West End. In a mature family business the relationship between professional management and shareholders is often one that has to be managed diplomatically. Fortunately in this case the shareholders were able to persuade the other directors that, given Foyles' heritage in Charing Cross Road the advantages of staying there would outweigh the disadvantages posed by the building and the management worked out a strategy for dealing with these disadvantages.

The redevelopment, of course, took far longer and cost far more than originally expected but in May 2014 Foyles moved from the premises it had occupied for some ninety years to the magnificently remodelled shop at 107 Charing Cross Road, which pretty much exactly matched the fourth of William's 1927 'Aims as a Bookseller': 'To have premises at least 100 feet long and 100 feet wide and, say, 50 feet high, with a gallery round and a glass dome roof...' Although a few customers (and this writer) feel some nostalgic regrets at the loss of the old shop, the new building has won many plaudits and several architectural awards and Foyles Charing Cross Road – with the slogan 'Welcome book lover, you are among friends' painted boldly across the central atrium – is once again, if not 'the World's Greatest Bookshop', at least up there with the very best.

Both the decision to relocate and the considerable investment involved are justified by the results. Five years after the opening of the new building, sales in the Charing Cross Road shop have increased by nearly 25%, even though the net sales space is slightly smaller. A couple of years after opening the new store we recruited a new chief executive, with considerable and relevant retailing experience. The staff training programme was developing excellent booksellers: he devised a general retail awareness module which was christened 'Barnum training', a reference to William's nickname, to give the booksellers additional retail skills.

The impact has been impressive: footfall, in spite of the disruption caused by the redevelopment of both our old site next door and Tottenham Court Road underground station, is some 10% higher than in the old shop and the fact that the sales growth has been significantly higher reflects the improvement in converting visitors to customers. I live in Camden only twenty minutes away and take great pleasure in entertaining visitors and friends in the Café, which occasionally leads to a guided tour. Each time I do so I delight in the vibrant atmosphere, the number of customers, more apparent than in the old shop because of the open-plan layout and the visibility and range of the books on offer. Good bookshops are about discovery and I discover new and eye-catching books on every visit.

Finally I felt that, not only had we truly saved and regenerated the business but that we had put in place a management team to take the company forward with only a very light touch needed from the shareholders.

11. EXIT

DURING THREE GENERATIONS OF FAMILY ownership the business had thrived, declined and been revived. Apart from short-term bank finance it had gone from my great-grandmother's kitchen table to an internationally known bookselling brand without a penny of outside investment. The professional management team of the last few years had begun to implement a coherent growth strategy relevant to the Foyles' brand, which could lead to a doubling or more of the size of the business. However, in early 2017 Christopher Foyle, as the major shareholder, decided that although the sales had grown by 200% since the death of Christina and the business was set on a steady growth path, the future of the company would be more secure if it were part of a larger organization.

The seeds of the eventual sale had been sown by William when he chose to give a majority shareholding to Christina, and those seeds assiduously cultivated by Christina when she decided to exclude the rest of the family from the management of the business. The result was that by the time she died and we of the next generation were heading towards retirement, our children had grown up with neither the expectation of being involved nor with the affection for 'Grandad's shop' which we had had. While William, the first chairman, had employed all his three children in the family business, Christina, having positioned herself as his natural successor, sidelined her two siblings. Although she later employed both my Foyle cousins, that employment only lasted a few years.

By the time Christina died William's great-grandchildren, who between them have all the skills necessary to supervise the running of the business, had made their career choices elsewhere. They had charted their own courses through life, as lawyers, entrepreneurs, in publishing and in the arts. The history of the family ownership has not been the usual 'clogs to clogs in three generations': if any of the present generations wear clogs it will be by design rather than of necessity. I suggested on several occasions that we bring onto the board some of the next generation, a Foyle cousin who works in publishing in Germany and one of my nephews who has shown considerable entrepreneurial skills in other fields, was rejected.

Had Christina, during her reign, continued to develop the business it could have become large enough to have professional management with hands-on family involvement being restricted to a non-executive board. But she didn't and it didn't and we, the third generation, have now sold the business. Since Christina's death we had put it back on a growth trajectory, tripling annual sales to nearly £30m, with more to come. The business strategy was there, the ongoing family ownership strategy wasn't; it was time for the Foyle family to disengage.

The sale process was of course not easy, lasting well over a year. The sadness and pain of selling the family business was exacerbated by the greed and in some cases incompetence of some of the professional advisers. I continue to be amazed by the many ways in which such a process can be complicated to justify the level of fees charged.

Eventually agreement was reached and after an exhaustive process the decision was taken to sell Foyles to the largest specialist bookselling chain in the UK, Waterstones, some thirty-five years after Christina had effectively gifted Tim

Waterstone his second shop. Waterstones has had its own roller-coaster ride but with its renewed commitment to excellence in bookselling and its financial muscle it is the ideal partner to implement Foyles' ambitious growth strategy. I am delighted that Grandad's shop, as I still think of it, is now in the hands of a dedicated bookseller.

Our final duty has been to ensure that the new owners respect and cherish the brand. I had tried to do so, as the brand was what remained of my beloved grandfather. My hope is that the new owners will nurture the business which, for our customers, represents a passion for good bookselling and an unrivalled knowledge of books. They have given undertakings to protect the Foyles brand and to keep its individuality as they have with other acquisitions, notably Hatchards in Piccadilly and Hodges Figgis in Dublin. We are passing on to them another strong brand, a thriving business which will, I believe, in due course make a significant contribution to their profits.

Although my time at Foyles has come to an end, I have my many memories. One will always stay with me: it is a musical memory, unconnected with books but saying much to me about the character of Foyles. In June 2016 the Foundation for Australia and New Zealand Arts, FANZA, which I helped set up and of which I was a trustee, had a New Zealand evening in Foyles' event space. One of the speakers, Witi Ihimaera, author of *Whale Rider*, came to the end of his talk and unexpectedly broke into the beautiful, lilting Maori love song, 'Pokarekare Ana', beloved of almost all New Zealanders. Soon the entire audience of 120 Kiwis joined in, including the then High Commissioner and his wife who was sitting beside me – they both have excellent voices and love singing. As I sat there while this gentle music swelled out into Charing Cross Road in the early summer evening I was reflecting that I had played a part in creating this lovely space where these things can happen, and feeling a sense of great joy – and pride - in my part in helping to rebuild Grandad's shop.

EPILOGUE

AT THE START OF THE 20th century my grandfather fell into bookselling by accident. Nearly 100 years later I did the same. This took me by surprise and led to a period so different from the rest of my life that I decided to write about it. I have found the writing to be both fun and therapeutic and it has prompted me to look back, as objectively as I can, on my life so far. I have tried to distil from seventy years and more of memories that fairly small part of me which has connected me to my family's business.

As we make our way through life we leave our marks on its walls, faint grey pencil scratches amid the swirling polychrome graffiti of history. Life leaves far greater marks on us, it moulds us, shapes us, changes us. It builds our carapace, with all its moss and scars and attitudes and family and relationships. I left hardly a mark on Kenya in the nine years I lived there: it played a huge part in shaping me. I had a greater impact on the Turks and Caicos Islands, a tiny nation where one person can make a difference, and it had a significant influence on me, preparing me for the breakdown of my first marriage. Writing this memoir has made me think about the part I have played in changing Foyles and more importantly the part Foyles has played in making and changing me. The former is fairly simple: together with others I have played a significant part in turning an old-fashioned and run-down family business into a vibrant central London destination with an appeal beyond just bookselling. In childhood the many enjoyable days spent in Foyles influenced my development in subtle ways. Of course they gave me a love of books and, through books, of travel, but there were other influences, equally important. The clientele of Foyles, sixty and seventy years ago, was a complete cross-section of British society plus a significant number of visitors from all over the world. All were there because of books and my young mind registered both that books are a great unifier and that the love of books was not restricted to people from my own culture.

More recently the ways in which Foyles changed me are far more obvious. Having spent much of my childhood at boarding school and of my adult life abroad, my friends were spread around the world. I hardly socialize locally and my non-working life centred largely on my family. From my comfortable home I still occasionally travelled abroad to work and although I loved London and for a couple of years had had a small pied-à-terre just off Charlotte Street I was not a Londoner. Other than the occasional meeting necessitated by my overseas work my visits to London were those of a tourist, to the theatre or an exhibition.

My involvement in Foyles and through it my involvement in the book trade has made me a Londoner, with all that entails. I socialize regularly with interesting and passionate people, I get involved in causes that matter to me, I get angry with things that are worth expending anger on and to the surprise of some of my oldest friends I read *The Guardian*. Being now a Londoner this no longer seems significant, but I recall driving through Hampshire in the heart of 'army officer' territory, calling into a village newsagent and asking for *The Guardian*. I was given a strange look and told 'we only get the one copy', as if it were obvious there was no demand.

I have also been able to give my time and support to

charities working in areas I care about: human rights, the environment and the arts. I have been able to encourage and support younger people who want to follow a similar path. When I see my children, rather than reminisce about the past which we can't change I tell them about my interest in things that can be changed. I have married a woman I met through Foyles, who shares my interests and passions, and with our shared involvements in books, the arts and related events we try to impart some of those passions to others. I have been lucky enough in my working life to be able to influence a few people; I thought that would finish with my retirement. Some years ago, before my involvement in Foyles, I was talking to my oldest daughter and bemoaning the fact that I no longer had influence, could no longer 'make a difference'. 'But Dad,' she said, 'you've influenced me and you've influenced my friends' and I was reminded that we change our world in tiny increments. Foyles has given me the opportunity to make a few more such tiny changes. My involvement with what was but is no longer my family's business has come to an end. I look back over the past twenty years and realize that such involvement has added a deep layer of richness to my life and has given me an understanding of myself that will colour and guide whatever I do from now on.

* * *

At the time of writing I retain an involvement in the book trade as a member of the board of the Booksellers' Association. This is an age when rapid changes in buying habits are devastating many areas of retail, bookselling as much as any. When Jeff Bezos set up Amazon he initially targeted bookselling not, I think, because he has a passion for books but because books are uniquely identifiable through the wonderful ISBN system and there can be no doubt in buyers' minds what they are ordering. Many bookshops have closed during the past twenty years or so. There are now only half as many independent bookshops as there were at the turn of the century. Fortunately during the past few years this trend has reversed and the number of independent bookshops in the UK is once again slowly growing. Most of those which have survived the shake-out are thriving and I believe that Foyles will also thrive, having become, once again, one of the finest destinations for booklovers anywhere in the world, with an unrivalled range of stock and a staff of exceptional booksellers.

*   *   *

We signed the sale agreement on the morning of 7 September 2018 and that afternoon I flew out to Sorrento with my wife and some of my family. I was grieving, feeling that part of my identity had been taken from me. But the following morning I was lying on a sunbed with the Mediterranean beneath me, a cold beer in my hand and Vesuvius across the bay and I thought if this is the rest of my life I guess I can cope. Foyles has been a large and very important part of me but not essential to my life and I realize that it did not define me, I can live without it in the knowledge that I have played my part in securing its future. Now, as I leave behind my links to the family business, links that go back to early childhood, I need to find out what does define me, or whether as humans we need to be defined.

Immediately after the sale, with 'moving on' in mind, I emailed four friends, all men, all a generation or so younger than me, all in their own way inspirational and with philanthropic leanings, none of whom know each other but each of whose friendship has been important to me. One lives in San Francisco, one in Taipei, one in Ramallah and one in London. I suggested that we get together sometime when they could coordinate their travel schedules and to my delight they all jumped at the opportunity. We met up in December 2018 at a house which I had rented for the weekend, just outside Salisbury, and from the moment I introduced them to each other the conversation flowed and new friendships were forged. After two days of good company, good food and good wine we have arranged to meet again later this year, this time in Ramallah, where we will plant olive trees for each member of our families on a plot of land. Each of my grandchildren will know that they own an olive tree in Palestine. I have no idea what will emerge from this, apart of course from some good olive oil, but whatever does, it will be positive and move me on to the next stage of my life.

April 2019

ACKNOWLEDGEMENTS

ABOVE EVERYTHING ELSE I OWE a huge debt of gratitude to my maternal grandfather William Foyle for the many ways in which he inspired me, above all for giving me an abiding love of books.

Huge thanks to all the staff at Foyles: it has been a privilege working with them. I have deliberately not named in this memoir any of the current staff, but would like now to say a few special thanks:

To Sharon Murray, the first general manager recruited after the death of Christina, who introduced some solid bookselling practices, who was a complete delight to work with and whose dedication to the wellbeing of the staff did much to bridge the gap between the owners and the workforce which had existed in Christina's time; to Mike McGinley who brought his considerable knowledge of wider retail and helped position the company for the 21st century; to Giles Armstrong, still going strong after more than 50 years working for Foyles (and the only member of staff to call me 'Sir'); to Paul Currie, Chief Executive in the years immediately preceding the sale, not a bookseller but a retailer to his fingertips, who made great efforts to understand William's ethos and innate retailing skills and who was brilliant at imparting his knowledge to the staff; and of course to Vivienne Wordley whose enthusiasm, effervescence and broad knowledge of marketing generally and the book trade in particular played such a large part in the re-energising of Foyles in the years after the death of Christina.

Thanks to the book-trade generally for encouraging us in our efforts to rebuild the business. It has been a surprise and a delight to find out how supportive an industry it is, how competitors and suppliers could also be friends. I suspect that is less common in other fields of retail. A portion of the proceeds from the sale of this book will go to The Booktrade Charity.

Many thanks to Colin Gant and Kathy Rentzenbrink, tutors on the Arvon Foundation memoir writing course at Lumb Bank, who gave me the confidence to get this memoir into print.

Thanks to Benjamin Buchan, whose editing skills have knocked some of the rough edges off my writing.

Thanks to Jamie Keenan for the cover design which captures some of the essence of The Shop as I have known it from childhood.

Special thanks to my three sisters Tina Bailey, Margaret Cox and Julie Cracknell, three delightful and in their own ways extraordinary ladies, who were utterly supportive in all I tried to do during my time working for our family's business.

And a second thank you, the biggest thank you of all, to Vivienne who, having made the transitions from colleague to friend to wife has been such an enormous source of support and guidance in all that I do. It is a great joy to spend my life with someone who shares my passions, not least my love of words.

The Book Trade Charity was established in 1837 and provides a wide range of support for current and past members of the booktrade. It also has affordable housing at The Retreat at Kings Langley and Bookbinders Cottages in Barnet, where new entrants to the trade who struggle to afford the cost of London housing mix with others who have retired.

Information at www.btbs.org

CPSIA information can be obtained
at www.ICGtesting.com
Printed in the USA
BVHW070708300721
613191BV00002B/384

9 781916 078215